MICHAEL H

CATILINE

HIS TURBULENT LIFE
HIS REVOLUTIONARY TIMES

Cover: Mural fresco of Catiline by Cesare Maccari, Palazzo Madama

Detail

© 2018

My books include: *Cellini* [a fully-revised 2018 edition], *Caravaggio* [a fully-revised 2018 edition], *Cesare Borgia, Renaissance Murders, TROY, Greek Homosexuality, ARGO, Alcibiades the Schoolboy, RENT BOYS, Buckingham, Homoerotic Art (in full color), Sailors and Homosexuality, The Essence of Being Gay, John (Jack) Nicholson, THE SACRED BAND, German Homosexuality, Gay Genius, SPARTA, Charles XII of Sweden, Mediterranean Homosexual Pleasure, CAPRI, Boarding School Homosexuality, American Homosexual Giants, X-rated HUSTLERS* and *Christ has his John, I have my George: The History of British Homosexuality*. I live in the South of France.

CONTENTS

PART I
The Founding of Catiline's Rome
Aeneas, Romulus and Remus, the first seven kings and the Roman Constitution
Page 4

PART II
Catiline's Heritage

≈≈

PART I

THE FOUNDING OF CATILINE'S ROME
AENEAS, ROMULUS AND REMUS, THE FIRST SEVEN
KINGS AND THE ROMAN CONSTITUTION

It began with Aeneas, the son of a Trojan warrior, who escaped Troy after its destruction by the Greeks, setting sail towards the western Mediterranean. On his way he stopped over at Carthage where he romanced Queen Dido, the Phoenician princess who had founded the city. Jilting her, Aeneas went on to found Rome, thereby sowing the seeds of future animosity between the two countries, mercantile Carthage and belligerent Rome. Aeneas showed the first of all Roman qualities, *virtus*, manliness, in penetrating Dido. In the future, each time Rome conquered a country, it would be seen as the ultimate in *virtus*, penetration, and every time a Roman demonstrated *virtus* by thrusting his sword into another man, he would be symbolically dominating him with his penis--from whence came the Roman distaste of being accused of passivity in the sex act, an accusation that would haunt Caesar himself up to the time of his death.

In my book *Troy* I have this to say about Aeneas' founding of Rome, a city cursed by Hera and Athena during the Trojan War, and cursed again when Aeneas abandoned Dido after taking his pleasure, two curses which produced, at times, deviant cowards the likes of Caligula, Nero, Commodus and others, just fit for Rome's dung heap:

> ''The survivors for years will roam the endless seas,
> Till coming to a western land of hills and trees.
> And there in pious memory of Troy of old,
> A mighty empire with naked hands will mold.
> But Hera and Athena's curse will waste their home;
> Into monstrous vice will descend eternal Rome''

Later noble Romans would claim to have had an ancestor on the boat with Aeneas, as today many Americans maintain that members of their own family had come over on the *Mayflower*. Aeneas and his men landed in Italy where they came upon the Rutulians, Etruscans led by a young prince, Turnus, who declared war against the Trojans because a neighboring king, Latinus, in answer to an oracle telling him to marry his daughter to a foreigner, offered her to Aeneas, although from infancy she had been promised to Turnus himself. Aeneas did battle at the side of his lover Pallas, a youth he educated, in the Greek way, in philosophy, in the use of weapons and in virtue. They were seconded by two other lovers, Nisus and Euryalus, about whom Virgil says, ''None were more beautiful.'' Euryalus was the younger, the belovèd. The night before the first battle against the Rutuli Nisus noticed that they had lowered their guard and so came up with a plan for a night attack. The young Euryalus, Virgil tells us, ''was dazzled, struck by a great desire for glory.''

5

But Nisus wished to preserve his belovèd, saying, "if chance or some god sweeps me to disaster, I want you to survive: your youth is more deserving of life. You must live to entrust me to the earth." Euryalus refused to be left behind and both went off to get Aeneas' permission to enter the enemy camp as, "the Rutulians are quiet, drowned in sleep and wine. If you allow us to seize the chance, you'll soon see us back again burdened with spoils after carrying out vast slaughter." Aeneas agreed and promised the boys a great reward: "If you truly manage to capture the camp, and take the scepter, you have seen the horse that Turnus rode, and the armor he wore, that same horse, the shield, and the crimson plumes will be your reward."

Virgil continues: "Leaving, they crossed the ditches, seeking the enemy camp in the shadow of night, destined yet to bring many deaths. They saw bodies in drunken sleep, stretched here and there on the grass ... Euryalus drove his sword into proud Rhamnes, who chanced to be breathing deeply in sleep ... Nisus killed three of the king's servants nearby, lying careless among their weapons ... He severed lolling necks with his sword, then struck off the head of their lord himself, and left the trunk spurting blood, the ground and the bed drenched with dark warm blood. Then came Serranus, noted for his beauty who had sported much that night and lay there limbs drowned by much wine ... others were attacked while they were unconscious ... Euryalus plunged his whole blade into Rhoetus' chest, and withdrew it red with death. Rhoetus choked out his life in dark blood and, dying, brought up wine mixed with gore ... Nisus said 'Let's go, since unhelpful dawn is near. Enough vengeance has been satisfied.' They left the camp and headed for safety.

"But they became lost and soon the Rutulians caught up with them. During the battle that ensued Nisus threw a spear 'through both of Tagus' temples, and fixed itself still warm in the pierced brain. Volcens, enraged, rushed at Euryalus with his naked sword.' Nisus, seeing his belovèd in mortal danger, shouted aloud, 'On me, Rutulians, turn our steel on me, me who killed Tagus. The guilt is mine, Euryalus neither dared nor had the power.' He was still speaking but the sword, powerfully driven by Volcens, passed through the ribs and tore the white breast of Euryalus who rolled over in death, the blood flowing down his lovely limbs, and his neck, drooping, sank on his shoulder, like a bright flower scythed, bowing as it dies, bending its weary head. Nisus rushed at Volcens but the enemy gathered around him in hand to hand combat, whirling his sword until he buried it full in the face of a shrieking Rutulian and, dying, robbed his enemy of life. Then, pierced through, he threw himself on the lifeless body of his belovèd, and found peace at last in the calm of death.''

Aeneas' lover Pallas took up the battle and confronted Turnus. ''Pallas threw his spear with all his might. The shaft flew and struck the top of Turnus' armor. At this, Turnus hurled his oak spear tipped with sharp steel. The spearhead, with a quivering blow, tore through the center of his shield, passed through all the layers of iron, of bronze, all the overlapping bull's hide, piercing the breastplate, and the mighty chest. Vainly Pallas pulled the hot spear from the wound: blood and life followed, by one and the same path. He fell in his own blood and he struck the hostile earth in death with gory lips.'' Aeneas pursued Turnus and then seized his chance: ''Seeing a favorable moment, he hurled his spear from a distance with all his might. Like a black hurricane the spear flew on bearing dire destruction, and pierced the outer circle of the seven-fold shield and hissing, passed through the center of Turnus' thigh. He sank, his knee bent beneath him, under the blow. 'I have earned this, I ask no mercy,' he said. 'I bid you to pity my old father and return me, or, if you prefer it, my body robbed of life, to my people. Take my fiancée Lavinia as your wife, don't extend your hatred further.' '' [Lavinia had been promised to Turnus and now the Rutulian offered to give her up to Aeneas, the problem being that Lavinia's mother, Amata, refused to accept Aeneas because she knew of his preference for boys.] Aeneas paused and might have shown mercy had he not seen Pallas' sword belt strapped to Turnus who now wore his enemy's emblems. ''As soon as Aeneas' eyes took in the trophy, a memory of cruel grief, blazing with fury and terrible in anger cried out: 'Shall you be snatched from my grasp, wearing the spoils of one who was my own? Pallas it is, Pallas who sacrifices you with this stroke and exacts retribution from your guilty blood.' So saying, burning with rage, he buried his sword deep in Turnus' breast. Turnus' limbs grew slack with death, and his life fled, with a moan, into the shadows." As Achilles had destroyed Hector, so Aeneas avenged Pallas.

Among Aeneas's many feminine conquests was a certain Roma who fell in love with the beauty of one of Aeneas's stopovers, a river surrounded by seven hills. She begged Aeneas to found a colony there, but when he refused she burned his ships during the night, stranding them on the site that would be named for her, Rome. Etruscans, however, maintain that the city owed its creation to the Etruscan word for today's Tiber River, *Rumon*, "river", the pronunciation of which Aeneas understood as Rome.

Another version of the founding of Rome came about with the birth of twin boys, Romulus and Remus, born in 753 B.C. to a woman who had been impregnated by the god Mars. The twins were stranded on the banks of the Tiber River when their grand-uncle, Amulius, heard a prophecy stating that they would kill him when they reached adulthood. Saved by a wolf who nursed them, a passing shepherd, Faustulus, raised them as his own. When they grew to manhood they did indeed murder Amulius, but during a quarrel the boys, whose hot blood was that of the War God, clashed over the future boundaries of the city, Remus mortally wounded by his brother, the first of the internecine devastation that would poison Rome throughout its history. Romulus gave his name to the new city.

Romulus and Remus on a Renaissance frieze and with the she-wolf.

Rome was ruled by seven kings, the first Romulus, the last Tarquin, a city modeled on the culture of the Greeks, adopting even the Greek Olympian godhead. Romans were also heavily inspired by the far more cultured Etruscans, from whom they learned trade and a deep love of luxury and sexual adaptability. Both Etruscan men and women took elaborate care of their bodies, shaven hairless, the men proud to show themselves naked, as did the woman, if not as often. Nights spent in drinking and lascivious discourse ended in intercourse where husbands shared their wives and took advantage of the wives of others, where youths and boys were especially sexually prized, and the resultant children were brought up without the slightest care of who fathered them. Vice did not exist among the Etruscans, just pleasure. Most historians believe the seven kings were of Etruscan origin, settlers who came from the ''north'', perhaps the Balkans, perhaps Asia Minor. They were noted experts in metal work, pottery and consummate merchants. Their first settlements were in Tuscany, in the towns of Etruria and Fiesole, both of which have their importance in our story.

Before Tarquin became king, he and his brother married sisters, the daughters of the reigning king Servius Tullius, but because the marriages were mismatches Tarquin killed his wife and his brother, and took his brother's wife for his own, as she had pleaded with him to do. They had three sons. This new wife, Tullia, encouraged Tarquin to now kill the seated king, Tullius, her father, which Tarquin did by hiring assassins who waylaid Servius in a street that became known as the Vicus Sceleratus, the Street of Crime. If this weren't enough, on her way home Tullia's chariot came upon the bloodied corpse of her father. When the driver stopped the chariot in horror, Tullia took the reins and drove the chariot over the body. Tarquin refused to bury it and those senators who protested were murdered.

Tarquin sent his son Sextus to capture a certain town. Before the besieged walls Sextus and his buddies camped out. While sharing a meal before their camp fire they discussed their sexual exploits, as boys are like to do, all the while vaunting the faithfulness of their wives. As proof, spies were sent out to each man's home, where all the wives were discovered in the arms of another, all except the wife of a certain Collatinus. Her virtue inflamed Sextus' desire, and after taking the town he decided to take the virtuous wife of his friend. She refused until Sextus swore he would tell Collatinus that he'd found her in bed with a slave. The deed done, she nonetheless confessed all to her husband and family before taking her life. This was the final straw that convinced Collatinus and his best friend, Brutus, to have the Senate end the kinship and replace it by joint Consuls, the first of whom were Collatinus and Brutus. They had Sextus assassinated, while Tarquin escaped to the court of King Aristodemus of Cumae, where he died in bed of natural causes.

The end of Tarquin [Lucius Tarquinius Superbus], in 509 B.C., saw the birth of the Roman Republic.

Rome knew wealth only through continued expansion, its first competitor the ancestors of Queen Dido, the woman jilted by Aeneas.

Rome and Carthage grew separately, the first becoming a military power made rich through conquest, the second gaining wealth through trade. Rome developed a unique attitude towards war: it would be total and Rome would never surrender. There would be no treaties until Rome had conquered its enemy, no matter how long such conquest took. The competition for the best political positions in Rome--Tribunes, senators, Consuls and such--was so ferocious that no general would risk the disapproval of his countrymen by accepting anything short of victory over an enemy. Rome's second asset (the first being all-out war) was its ability to incorporate subjected countries, sending Roman citizens to colonize them as well as accepting native populations into the Roman flock, thanks to which Rome gained a nearly inexhaustible source of goods and manpower.

The Carthaginians, seeing Romans as potential bullies, honored them early on. Already, in 351 B.C., they gave Rome the gift of a huge crown of pure gold weighing 11 kilos, a gift so prized by the Romans that they put it in their most sacred Temple, Jupiter Optimus Maximus on the Capitoline Hill. Romans and Carthaginians were then so close that they considered themselves citizens of each other's country.

But Roman might took a jump ahead as the Romans extended their power over both northern and southern Italy. To the south was Magna Graecia, an area inhabited by Greek colonists. Rome destroyed the power of its leader, Pyrrhus, during a series of battles that Pyrrhus usually won, but at such severe cost to him that the total of his wins culminated in a huge loss of men and material, from whence comes today's expression, a Pyrrhic Victory. Pyrrhus returned to Greece where, during a battle, an old woman knocked him unconscious by throwing a tile from a rooftop, allowing his capture and beheading. Thanks to Roman victories, other nations began to fear Rome, among them Egypt where the Greek ruler Ptolemy initiated diplomatic relations between the two countries.

It is not my place, after a hiatus of nearly 3000 years, to make the slightest judgement on what might, or might not, be myth, legend or truth concerning Aeneas, Romulus, Remus and the existence of the early kings.

Between the first seven kings and the establishment of an empire, there was a brief period called the Republic. When the Republic fell, Rome basically reverted back to the times of the first kings, who were now called emperors. The Senate had been a rubber stamp under the kings, its function to elect new kings, as under the Empire it elected new emperors, although an emperor could designate the man who would fill his shoes, normally by first adopting him and then bestowing on him the title of Caesar. There were nonetheless occasions when the army decided who would become emperor, as in the case of Claudius.

At the outset armies were recruited from the landed classes, the rich providing horses and horsemen, while poor farmers made up the light infantry. Service could last between a few weeks to a few months, giving men time to return to their farms for harvests and replantation. The war against Carthage saw duty stretched into years, and with victories in outer provinces a soldier could be called away for from five to ten years. During this time, their farms fell into ruin and were bought up by patricians who turned them into estates for commercial farming, the war-time profits immense, especially as the farms were manned by slaves brought in thanks to victories over peoples outside of Rome. Deprived of land and its income, soldiers depended more and more on their generals to fulfill their needs, generals who gained limitless power thanks to their men, the very basis of the success of Sulla, Pompey and Caesar. Sulla had recognized the potential of Pompey when he first met the very young general. He rose from his seat to greet him, "a singular honor", writes Adrian Goldsworthy in his book *In the Name of Rome*, that "he notably failed to extend to many more distinguished men."

Another surprise was the existence of a Roman Constitution, because before the 18th century there were extremely few others. The Constitution was a patchwork of customs, traditions and laws, some written, many not, and like the American Constitution, patterned after that of Rome, it was vague enough to allow various interpretations. Like most things Roman, Roman laws too had their origin with the Greek lawmaker and statesman Solon, laws that the Romans acquired from the Greek colonies of the Magna Graecia in the South of Italy. The laws were codified into Twelve Tables around 450 B.C. and probably destroyed by invading Gauls in 387, one of the many reasons Caesar had the Gaul general Vercingetorix throttle to death in the Roman Forum [described in the chapter on Caesar].

The Constitution originated during the times of the first seven kings, evolved under the Republic, and spanned the years of Empire. The most amazing characteristic of the Constitution were the checks and balances, the veritable heart of the success of the American Constitution. Assemblies composed of the people elected magistrates, accepted or rejected laws, administered justice and declared war or peace. The magistrates had the right to call up and preside over assemblies, and one magistrate could often veto another. Caesar came to realize that the Constitution's demand for checks and balances made Rome ungovernable. The only way out was the restitution of the institutions of the first seven kings, which would indeed take place following Caesar's assassination, under the title of emperors, as mentioned above, the first being Augustus. For Republicans like Cato, Brutus and Cicero, the greater good would be best served by finding better men and passing better laws, under Rome's existing, highly malleable Constitution, which led Brutus to assassinate Caesar. But Brutus died in battle, Cato committed suicide, and Cicero was beheaded.

Caesar.

Caesar, despite having the deaths of perhaps 2 million soldiers and others on his conscience, was universally described as lavishly generous, humane, good natured, a devoted friend, always ready to give, to relieve and to pardon.

PART II

CATILINE'S HERITAGE
THE PUNIC WARS

Catiline was born into an empire created a mere forty years earlier with the defeat of the greatest commercial and exploratory power the world had ever known, Carthage, Carthage that should have shunned everything Roman after Aeneas' virile conquest of its queen, Dido, on his way to founding the city of the seven hills.

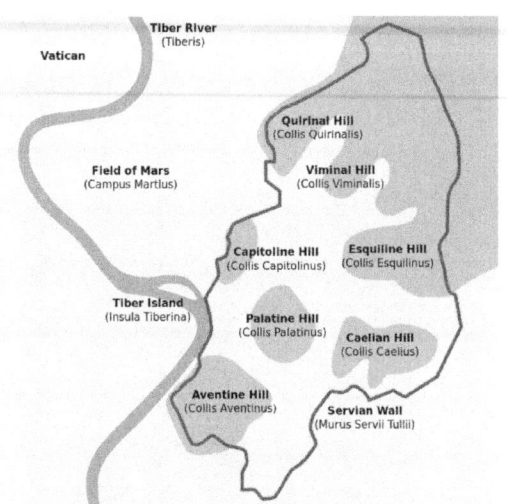

The Seven Hills of Rome

Rome and Carthage grew separately, the first becoming a military power made rich through conquest, the second gaining wealth through trade. Rome developed a unique attitude towards war: it would be total and Rome would never surrender. There would be no treaties until Rome had conquered its enemy, no matter how long such conquest took. The competition for the best political positions in Rome--Tribunes, senators, Consuls and such--was so ferocious that no general would risk the disapproval of his countrymen by accepting anything short of victory over an enemy. Rome's second asset [the first being all-out war] was its ability to incorporate subjected countries, sending Roman citizens to colonize them as well as accepting native populations into the Roman flock, thanks to which Rome gained a nearly inexhaustible source of goods and manpower.

The Carthaginians, seeing Romans as potential bullies, honored them early on. Already, in 351 B.C., they gave Rome the gift of a huge crown of pure gold weighing 11 kilos, a gift so prized by the Romans that they put it in their most sacred Temple, Jupiter Optimus Maximus on the Capitoline Hill. Romans and Carthaginians were then so close that they considered themselves citizens of each other's country.

But Roman might took a jump ahead as the Romans extended their power over both northern and southern Italy. To the south was Magna Graecia, an area inhabited by Greek colonists. Rome destroyed the power of its leader, Pyrrhus, during a series of battles that Pyrrhus usually won, but at such severe cost to him that the total of his wins culminated in a huge loss of men and material, from whence comes today's expression, a Pyrrhic Victory. Pyrrhus returned to Greece where, during a battle, an old woman knocked him unconscious by throwing a tile from a rooftop, allowing his capture and beheading. Thanks to Roman victories, other nations began to fear Rome, among them Egypt where the Greek ruler Ptolemy initiated diplomatic relations between the two countries.

Aroused by the immense financial gain and the equally immense military glory that came through conquest, Rome was quick to answer an appeal from Sicily for help fighting mercenaries expatriated from Magna Graecia when Pyrrhus sailed back to Greece. An appeal had also been sent to Carthage who coveted Sicily, hoping it would become the center of their trading empire. Carthage answered by sending a fleet to Sicily. They attempted to keep the Romans from leaving the Italian port of Rhegium and landing on the island, their general Hanno promising that Carthaginian ships would prevent the Romans from even washing their hands in the sea. Rome nonetheless gained control over the eastern segment of Sicily, leaving the western part to Carthage. Hanno was crucified for not keeping his word.

The Romans, comfortable only during land battles, had a fleet, but nothing in comparison to the Carthaginians'. They therefore set in motion a massive building campaign under the leadership of the Consul Duilius. The ships were unwieldy but possessed crows, a Roman invention, long and narrow bridges equipped with spikes and held in an upward position on the prows of the Roman ships until released when the enemy ship was approached. A pointed spike was then driven into the enemy deck and held fast by the weight of the bridge, over which the Roman soldiers stormed, as they would during a battle on land. During an initial encounter with the Carthaginians, off the coast of Sicily, the Carthaginian sailors literally snickered at the sight of their

Roman counterpart, so certain were they of victory over a fleet of tyros. They lost and their commander was crucified, while Duilius went on to Rome where he was honored with Rome's highest honor, a Triumph. The Romans, emboldened, then sailed on to pester Sardinia and Corsica.

The Carthaginians, unlike the Romans, depended heavily on mercenaries. They now sent to Sparta for the general Xanthippus to help them in Sicily. At the same time, the Romans, emboldened by their naval successes, decided to invade north Africa, only the second time they had ever left Italy, the first being the invasion of Sicily. They were victorious until a storm sank nearly 300 of their ships, with the loss of thousands of men. The Carthaginians too had victories in Sicily until, during one attack, the Romans took special care to wound the Carthaginian elephants. The animals, made mad with fear at seeing and hearing their fellow elephants cry out in pain, turned to retreat, trampling the Carthaginians and their mercenaries underfoot. Thirty thousand were thought to have died. The Roman commander, Metellus, later went to Rome for his Triumph, parading the elephants he had captured, through the narrow streets of the city. Back in Sicily his Carthaginian counterpart was put to death, replaced by Hamilcar Barca who was not so much expected to take back the island from the Romans as to save what he could. When he failed, Carthage sued for peace. The terms were terrible: Sicily would be evacuated, all Roman prisoners freed, and an indemnity of 3,200 talents was to be paid, 1,000 immediately, the rest over a period of 10 years. In this way the First Punic War came to an end. [Punic, a Latin word, refers to peoples of Phoenician descent.]

After the war a great period of instability ensued. Mercenaries returning to Carthage revolted when not paid. The Carthaginians had attempted to control the mercenaries by recruiting them from different nationalities so that they literally couldn't speak the same language; the mercenaries were dispersed throughout north Africa in small groups to keep them from uniting their forces; and their women and children were often taken hostage. The mercenaries nonetheless revolted. Battles of incredible cruelty followed wherein captives on both sides were tortured, their hands cut off and their legs broken, they were suffocated with their own genitals or buried alive, while others were nailed to a cross. Rome took advantage of the chaos by taking definitive control of Sardinia and Corsica. Hamilcar Barca chose that moment to lead his men to Spain. The Carthaginian fleet was in such poor repair that Hamilcar was forced to march on foot to the Pillars of Hercules where they crossed over to Spain. Hamilcar founded New Carthage, perfectly positioned for fishing and trade, and an excellent port for the expedition of silver that Carthaginian slaves extracted from nearby mines. Hamilcar turned the reins of power over to his son, Hannibal, a man described by the historian Livy as reckless in courting danger, indefatigable, sleeping on the ground wrapped in his cloak, always first to attack and last to leave the battlefield.

Hannibal expanded the size of his empire until he controlled half of the peninsula. His mines produced 135 kilos of silver a day, making New Carthage rich. With an infantry of 60,000 and a cavalry of 8,000, he didn't hesitate to attack neighboring Saguntum, a town that immediately appealed to Rome for help. As Rome took its time in deciding the fate of the city, many of the inhabitants committed mass suicide, others surrendered. Hannibal shared the town's spoils with his soldiers and set aside the town's gold and silver for future use. Rome sent an embassy to Carthage demanding the return of Saguntum. When Carthage refused, Rome declared war.

Hannibal Barca 47 B.C.- c. 181 B.C.

As Hannibal made his plans to invade Italy, a dangerous scheme because he would have to pass through the lands of hostile tribes as well as traverse the Pyrenees and the Alps, the Roman Longus led 22,000 other men and a fleet of 160 in an attack on Carthage. The tables had now been turned, as Rome, a former land power, reigned supreme over the seas, obliging Carthage and Hannibal to rely on a land army. Hannibal's forces consisted of 12,000 men, many of them mercenaries. Carthage requested help from the south of Italy, from Magna Craecia. Greece and Carthage had a long history of friendship and trade. Hannibal had been taught Greek history and literature by Greek tutors hired by Hannibal's father Hamilcar. In addition, it was the Greek Alexander the Great who had first used elephants in battle, 480 of them in his campaign in Syria. The Romans considered elephants as being untrustworthy, and indeed, when panicked they often turned on their own troops in an attempt to escape injury. For this reason their drivers were equipped with mallets carved to a sharp point that they drove into the elephant's spinal cord when the animal rebelled. Hannibal also engaged Celts from Gaul and the Po Valley, savages he considered appropriate cannon fodder, but men who knew how to fight.

To put an end to Hannibal, Rome nominated two new generals and supplied them with 87,000 troops, compared to Hannibal's 50,000. The two armies came together at the town of Cannae. In face of the better-trained and more experienced Carthaginians and their mercenaries, as well as the far superior Celtic horsemen, 70,000 Roman soldiers were killed and another 10,000 captured. On the battlefield the Roman wounded, mad with thirst and suffering from severe wounds, bared their necks to the blade of the enemy, begging for release. Livy tells us that some went so far as to bury their heads in the soil in an attempt to suffocate themselves. One Carthaginian mercenary was pulled from under a Roman soldier, his ears and nose torn off: the Roman, having lost his weapon, had bitten at his enemy with his teeth.

Thanks to his victory, Hannibal knew the time was right to send his brother Mago to Carthage for reinforcements. Mago shocked the Carthaginian Council by emptying, on the floor, the contents of a huge sack, the gold rings taken from the thousands of dead Romans slaughtered at Cannae. Hannibal's request for more troops was granted. Hannibal, after seven years of fighting in Italy, then rode to the very gates of Rome. The alarm was such that the Romans resurrected a ritual extinct for a hundred years: they sacrificed two men and two women to the gods, Gauls and Greeks, all four buried alive.

Back in Spain, a new general, the soon-to-be-famous Publius Cornelius Scipio, age 25, was made commander. He had studied Hannibal's tactics and he had spread the word that he was the son of Zeus, Zeus who had impregnated Scipio's mother in the form of a snake, the form he preferred when not entering the spread thighs of a woman disguised as the head and neck of a swan. Scipio attacked and conquered New Carthage. He made friends of the New Carthaginians by freeing the population, and great wealth for Rome by capturing the silver mines. Hannibal's second brother, Hasdrubal, who had failed to save New Carthage, took his remaining troops to Italy to join Hannibal. His other brother Mago was killed on the way, as was Hasdrubal whose head, in a gesture of infamous cruelty, was decapitated and thrown into Hannibal's lines, the way in which Hannibal learned of his brother's slaying. Another piece of bad news came his way: Scipio had been sent to destroy Carthage.

The bust of Scipio Africanus in the the Naples National Archaeological Museum.

Scipio started off by launching a surprise attack on a camp outside the city during the night, setting its wood and reed dwellings on fire. Sixty-three thousand men perished. Carthage immediately sued for peace. The terms were draconian: all prisoners would be released and Italian deserters put to death, all Carthaginian armies would be withdrawn from Spain, Italy and Gaul, all islands between Italy and Africa would be abandoned, the entire Carthaginian navy would be handed over, except for ten ships, and an indemnity of 10,000 talents would be paid to cover the war damage--but Carthage would not be razed. The ships were burned in the waters in front of Carthage and deserters, their former allies, had their throats cut in full view of Carthaginians. The Second Punic War came to an end and Scipio rose to near godhood, known for all time as Scipio Africanus.

Hannibal, after an amazing span of 15 years in Italy, fled to Asia Minor where he helped one prince after another in their wars against Rome. Finally cornered in Bithynia, homeland of Antinous, he took his life with poison.

Although Romans considered themselves pious and courageous, they were especially jealous of any other power around what they called ''our sea''. The historian Cato, who had taken part in the First Punic War, hated the Carthaginians so ferociously that he used every occasion to condemn them as future predators. The Senate sent him to Carthage to see if the population was as downtrodden as Carthaginian emissaries claimed they were. Cato discovered a city spilling over with wealth, whose citizens were vigorous and whose fighting men strong and outstandingly armed. He returned to Rome to warn of the danger, ending each of his speeches with the chilling words, Carthage must be destroyed!

The casus belli for Roman intervention was an attack by neighboring tribes on a stretch of fertile farmland owned by Carthage. The tribes begged for Rome to intervene, which it did by sending an embassy that, after viewing the situation, voted in favor of the tribes. Not only would Carthage be forced to render the land, but the city would also have to turn over all its arms, enough to equip an estimated 20,000 men. Carthage complied. Unarmed, Rome revealed the secret second part of its plan: Carthaginians could live under their own laws, but not under the skies over Carthage. The city had to be obliterated, along with its harbors and ships. The Romans pushed their bad faith so far as to assure the Carthaginians that as an exclusively agricultural nation they would be better off, since it was their ships and commerce which had been the cause of their troubles up to then.

The Carthaginians begged for a month's grace during which they could send their own embassy to Rome to plead their cause. They chose the general Hasdrubal to lead them and then, unknown to Rome, they proceeded to murder every Italian within their walls. Still in the dark, the Romans granted them a thirty-day truce that the Carthaginians used to produce weapons. Each available space was turned into a workshop dedicated to producing swords, shields, spears and other arms. Even ships were built from whatever scrap could be unearthed.

Faced with a city again powerful, the Romans answered by sending a teenager to head their armies, a boy called Scipio Aemilianus, Scipio Africanus' son--a boy, perhaps, but one with the Scipio name and, hopefully, the Scipio touch.

The battle for Carthage followed the usual form of others in the ancient world: naval blockades, the construction of a mole, breaching towers; captives, Roman and Carthaginian, inhumanly butchered in sight of their fellow citizens; the final entry during which the Romans went from street to street, door to door, raping, maiming, killing and burning. Perhaps 50,000 Carthaginians were taken prisoner and sold into slavery. Hasdrubal and other dignitaries were spared.

Hasdrubal's wife saw her people defend their town from the balconies and roofs above the winding streets, throwing down stones and tiles on the invaders. But the houses were engulfed, like a wind-crazed fire, by the vengeful Romans who murdered and pillaged, taking as loot women, stripping children naked and lashing them to carts like beasts of burden, forcing them under whip to return to the beaches with loads of loot. Many of the survivors, losing heart, jumped from the walls. Their children, those who collapsed on the trails to the ships, were left to die or went mad. Yet a few made it to the surrounding woods where the Romans feared to pursue.

The runaways would return to the smoldering remains of their citadel on the days to follow, once the enemy had taken to the seas. The were too late to save their dead relatives from the horror of being mutilated by birds and animals, their bodies torn to pieces and devoured, their final resting place the belly of the beast. These would never know purification by incorruptible fire, or entrance into the Underworld, gateway to the Afterworld. These would have no burial mound to be honored by family and loved ones and passers-by. These would vanish from human memory, the most horrifying damnation known to Romans and Carthaginians alike.

For the survivors worse still was to come in the form of plague. This was neither instant death nor resurrection thanks to the funeral pyre. This came with a burning of the head and a bleeding of the throat, with pain in the chest and retching of the stomach, with pustules and ulcers and stinking flesh, with voiding bowels and feverish insanity. These even vultures did not venture to eat. The devout who raised pyres in accordance with eternal laws saw them stolen by those who got to them first with their own dead, or saw bodies thrown on the pyres where other cadavers were already in flame.

Lawlessness broke out, the strong plundered the weak, and with loss of heart came loss of belief in the mercy of the gods. Licentious acts of bestiality robbed Carthaginians of the last strands of unity that had held them together as a people. In straggly groups they wandered off, abandoning the city to the dust of ages.

After the fall of Carthage, complained Sallust, virtue and loyalty were exchanged for the quest of money and power, the true marks of distinction and renown, and poverty became a disgrace, honor and modestly gave way to avidity, luxury, lasciviousness, jealousy, covetousness, robbery and murder, "men prostituted themselves like women", continued Sallust, "and women sold their chastity to every comer. They went to bed before they needed sleep, and instead of waiting until they were hungry, thirsty or cold, they forestalled their bodies' needs by self-indulgence." Young men resorted to any means in order to procure sensual pleasures, even crime.

PART III

SULLA
AND MITHRIDATES

Quite naturally Catiline traced his ancestry back to Aeneas, and there had been a number of Consuls in his lineage, something Catiline strove for over a long period of years, without success, certainly the catalyst for his decision to take Rome by other means. The Catiline family had fallen on hard times, declining both socially and financially. His father was Lucius Sergius Silus, his mother Belliena.

Catiline's schooling was much the same as other well-bred Roman lads, consisting of as much math as necessary to function in the market, rhetoric, syntax and literature based on Latin and Greek. Catiline's literary sources were Homer, of course, and Horace and Virgil. He most probably also studied the Greeks, Aristotle, Socrates, Plato, Euripides and Aristophanes.

Catiline entered the army in 90 B.C., probably as an officer thanks to the influence, albeit waning, of his family. The commander was Pompeius Strabo, his first battle against the Italic people known as the Samnites, who were fighting for Roman citizenship, a battle they would ultimately win, although not this time, brought to heel by a new young officer, Lucius Cornelius Sulla in 88 B.C., two years following Catiline's enlistment. Of immense importance in our story, we will now pause to study Sulla in detail.

Sulla was so loved by his soldiers that he received the Grass Crown, the highest and rarest of military honors, awarded by the men in his army for extreme bravery, a crown made of grass, flowers and whatever else the soldiers collected from a battlefield, and presented to their commander. The Roman Senate, for its part, thanked Sulla for his soldiering by sending him off to quench the ardors of King Mithridates VI of Pontus, in Phrygia, a plum as he and his soldiers would be able to plunder some of the world's richest cities.

Sulla was loved by his soldiers, was said to have been charming and, like Caesar, benefited from great luck, which implied divine favor. He possessed but one testicle.

Mithridates was one of the most fascinating villains known to humanity. His birth had been announced by a comet, the brightness of which obscured even the sun. His father had built up a huge army of locals from Cappadocia, Phrygia, Pontus and Greece, and soon controlled the entire southern shore of the Black Sea. When his father was assassinated by his wife who ruled in favor of her younger son, Mithridates' brother, Mithridates was forced to flee the capital Amaseia. While his mother made friends with the Romans, Mithridates reinforced those who had fled with him with mercenaries from Crete and Gaul, and Galatians from the highland of Anatolia who fought stark naked. Returning to Amaseia, he had his mother and younger brother thrown into a dungeon and left to starve. He married his sister and founded his own dynasty. A superb horseman and archer, he exercised daily, endowing himself with an anatomy he so admired that he had armor shaped to capture the exact contours of his abs and pectorals, a copy of which he sent to Delphi to be admired by the god Apollo--an expert in boys' abs and pectorals, among other anatomical points of interest.

Since Rome was an ever-invasive power, and as Roman legions were as hopeless on water as they were valiant on land, Mithridates decided to build a navy. The navy became an obsession, as did his belief that, like his father, he would be poisoned. He prepared himself for the eventuality by taking small daily doses of poison. Both precautions--a navy and the gradual development of an antidote--saved his life and his kingdom. His sister-wife, in the fashion of his mother, tried to poison him in order to place their eight-year-old son on the throne. She too was immured. When the Romans saw that Mithridates was gaining increasing power by bringing Bithynia, the homeland of Antinous [Hadrian's boy] and King Nicomedes [whose boy was Caesar when he was young], to his side, and by overpowering the Scythians, an act of war that even Cyrus the Great and Alexander the no-less Great had failed to accomplish, the Romans sent troops to douse his ardors. While they were on their way, Mithridates used the time to bring Cappadocia over to his side. He did so by requesting a meeting with the king of Cappadocia. As Mithridates was feared, the king had him intimately searched before being allowed access. Mithridates is said to have stopped the searcher from going too far by noting, when the man placed a hand on his groin, that he didn't share the man's pederastic tastes. Once inside the room he withdrew a knife lodged between his thighs and bled the king like a pig. He then made certain that his allies would be fully bound to him by committing an act that the Romans would never forgive. He sent secret messages to every corner of Asia Minor, ordering the peoples to destroy all Romans in their midst, 80,000 men, women and children. Such was the hatred for Italians that in some places parents were obliged to witness the slaughter of their children, then men the slitting of their wives' throats before their own deaths, often by suffocating on their own genitals. Roman slaves were freed and half of all the debts the peoples had owed the Romans was forgiven, the other half went to Mithridates. He dealt with the rulers of provinces that he was unsure of in a way adopted by Renaissance tyrants and by the mafia hundreds of years later: they were invited to a banquet during which the doors were locked, permitting Mithridates' men to kill them all.

Rome sent legions to deal with the king once and for all. Most of the commanders, avenging the death of the 80,000, showed no mercy as they went from one of Mithridates' client countries to another, raping, massacring and stealing anything of value, burning everything that wasn't. One young commander earned the sobriquet *"carnifex adulescens"*, "teenage butcher". He was none other than Gnaeus Pompeius Magnus, known to us as Pompey, later Pompey the Great, Caesar's greatest future adversary. Some commanders spared towns if they gave up immediately, knowing that it was the best way to save the lives of their troops. As many leaders had been murdered in the mafia-style dinners, the towns were more than happy to go over to Rome. One noted holdout surprised the Romans by releasing bears and wasps on them as the Romans attempted to tunnel under the walls.

His back up against the wall, Mithridates ordered his harem to commit suicide by taking poison. One member, the mother of one of his sons, chose to have her throat cut by a eunuch while wearing the royal diadem. [Eunuchs were capable of having erections despite the loss of their testicles, so they were often obliged to have the penis severed at the root.] Mithridates too took poison, but due to years of building up a resistance to it, he was forced to ask a servant to give him eternal release by the sword.

Back in Rome Caius Marius, who had won six consulships, decided to relieve Sulla of his command. He was aided by Publius Sulpicius Rufus, a Tribune. Not at all in agreement, Sulla returned to Italy and marched on Rome, the first time in its history. Marius and Sulpicius fled and Sulla declared them both enemies of the people, putting a price on their heads. Sulpicius was murdered by one of his slaves whom Sulla immediately freed and paid the agreed award. Sulla then ordered the slave pushed off the Tarpeian Rock, to his death. This seems a strange sequence of events, but it was in holding with Roman law: a promise was made and kept, and only then did the slave pay for betraying his master, the penalty under Roman law. In the same way, a virgin girl could not be put to the sword. So in order to decimate an enemy's family, his virgin daughters were raped and *then* killed. Sulla returned to the East to stabilize things there and a certain senator, Cornelius Asiaticus, was elected consul. He tried to replace Sulla as the leading power in Rome but when Sulla threatened to return with his legions, Asiaticus met with him and offered him full powers. Then, on returning to Rome, Asiaticus repudiated his promises. War broke out between Rome and Sulla who declared that any supports of Asiaticus would be severely dealt with. Pompey himself, the ''teenage butcher'', threw in his lot with Sulla. Sulla's forces were victorious during the ensuing Battle of Colline Gate, at which 50,000 soldiers on both sides lost their lives. Sulla gathered 9,000 prisoners and herded them into the Circus Maximus where, in the presence of senators and the general public, he went over the fine points of his assuming ultimate power in Rome, while down below the prisoners, screaming for mercy, had their throats slit or swords thrust into their chests, in sound and view of Sulla, the senators, Rome's nobility and everyone else. He was named dictator [*dictator rei constituendae*, dictator to restore the Republic], a position granted him by the Consuls who had had no other choice.

By garrisoning Rome, Sulla destroyed the Republic, an act Caesar would later repeat, the justification for his armed entry into Rome, followed by civil war, Caesar's assassination, and the enthronement of his adopted son and Rome's first emperor, Augustus.

To these dead Sulla added 1,500 more from the nobility, some of whom were senators. Their wealth was naturally confiscated, making Sulla and his supporters rich beyond belief. The sons and grandsons of the victims were banned from political office, a penalty that was in place for 30 years. Then he doubled the number of senators from 300 to 600, the vast majority his close friends.

Yet Sulla soon resigned the dictatorship and had himself elected consul. He dismissed his guards and walked the streets of

Rome accompanied only by his friends and supporters [his clients, as they were referred to in Rome].

Sulla.

Catiline learned that he too could give way to his penchant for despotic power, especially as a means of escaping poverty and the obscurity of his parents and recent ancestors, although the first had been men of renown. He could fulfill his desire for money and luxury, both of which appear to not have been the goals of Sulla, even if both were the reality of Sulla's existence, the natural benefits of his victories in battle and his dictatorship. What saved Catiline was his generosity, his willingness to share his wealth and the fruits of his climb to power with his followers, a part of the reason why they were devoted to him.

In character it was said of Sulla that he was ''no better friend, no worse enemy.'' He was extremely generous to his companions and allies. Noted for his good looks when young, he was a womanizer and was rumored, throughout his military career, to have had numerous male paramours. As Adrian Goldsworthy writes in his wonderful book, *Caesar*, Sulla ''was believed to be very active sexually, taking both men and women as lovers.'' When he left Rome definitively he was accompanied by actors, prostitutes and rent-boys, along with a longtime favorite, the actor Metrobius, with whom he organized orgies at his villa outside Rome, an invitation open to every boy, youth and handsome man, in the total absence of women. Plutarch writes: ''Although

Metrobius was past the age of youthful bloom, Sulla remained to the end of his life in love with him, and made no secret of the fact.'' Sulla, despite the thousands he had executed, died in bed, surrounded by the hundreds he had entertained, but was made to pay for his massacres by ''falling prey to a disease which caused his flesh to rot and his body to be covered with lice-infected sores,'' states Sallust.

PART IV

THE SENATE, CONSULS AND TRIBUNES, PATRICIANS AND PLEBEIANS
THE GRACCHI BROTHERS AND GAIUS MARIUS

The Italic peoples were Rome's allies, and against huge opposition they won Roman citizenship in a law known as the Lex Julia, the Julian Law, introduced by Julius Caesar in 90 B.C., when Catiline was 19. The law became part of the Roman Constitution, which needs explaining, as do the offices of those who ran the Republic, the first of which was the Senate.

The Senate derived its name from the Latin *senex*, old man, generously interpreted as an assembly of elders. Ancient history maintains that it was Romulus who nominated the first senators, 100 in number. It was the most permanent of all Roman institutions, the only institution that has survived to this day. Under the first Roman kings the Senate was an advisory council, which nonetheless elected the next king, and it was the Senate that deposed the last king, Tarquin. The power of the Senate waxed and waned during the Republic. With the death of Caesar and the assumption of Augustus, the Senate was dominated by emperors, becoming, once again, an advisory council.

During the reign of the kings, Senate members were chosen by the king himself, men of experience to guide him, drawn from the best of the nobility, a *rex* who would perpetuate their interests. The Senate nominated a new king and sent the name to an assembly that confirmed it, after which the Senate validated the assembly's confirmation. [Otherwise, the early assembly was responsible for mostly family affairs, such as adoptions and the validation of wills.] During the Republic the purpose of the Senate was to counsel two Consuls chosen by the Plebeian Tribune [to be discussed]. Because the Consuls were elected for only one year, while the Senate went on eternally, the Senate had, in the long term, the greater powers, although the Consuls also had immense powers, as we'll see. [Due to the importance of Consuls, Tribunes and the Senate, only their titles will be capitalized.]

Senators did not sit in a semicircle around an open space, but rather in straight and parallel lines on each side of the building, the Curia Julia.

The highest office of the Roman Republic was held by two Consuls, elected by the Centuriate Assembly made up of all Romans [one Centuriate voter representing from 100 to 200 Roman citizens]. Only the Centuriate Assembly could declare war and it was also the highest court of appeal, especially concerned with major crimes such as treason. It could grant *imperium*, the absolute protection of the holder, in the case of Consuls they were each granted 12 lictors, personal bodyguards. Consuls held their office for one year, their historical powers ending with the death of Caesar and the founding of the Roman Empire under all-powerful emperors. In times of peace the Consuls held administrative, legislative and judicial powers, and in time of war they held the highest military commands. Consuls had the power to interpret auguries, essential in leading armies in the field, as favorable results gave soldiers courage and near invulnerability, a little like African shamans promising warriors immunity from bullets. Each Consul could veto the actions of the other Consul. At first limited to patricians, plebeians were eventually also elected Consuls. After a consulship the former Consul would be rewarded with a lucrative governorship somewhere in the provinces, a guarantee of wealth thanks to the taxes he could impose, the possessions he could steal and the business opportunities he could initiate in his behalf. Apparently, only Cicero made of point of not looting the territory of his governorship following his term as Consul, which he never tired of reminding his audiences. Speaking of Cicero, Caesar's heir Octavian suggested they share a consulship, he and Cicero, which made Cicero smile because Consuls had to be 42, while Octavian, the future Emperor Augustus, was 19.

Senate members were chosen from the well-born, although under Sulla there were major reforms. Sulla detested rule by the people, and lamented the gradual loss of power by the Senate, in favor of plebeian Tribunes, Tribunes originally established to protect the people, plebeians, from mistreatment from patricians. As a patrician Sulla set about reinforcing the senators' influence, but when he obtained dictatorial powers [to be discussed] he invaded Rome at the head of his soldiers, a desecration of the Constitution that was the visible proof of how little the Senate counted in reality, and how much the power and destiny of Rome depended on its generals and armies. In wanting to strengthen the Senate, Sulla's use of force undermined it permanently, and even though he eventually retired to his country estates, the harm had been done and precedent established, to be later used by Caesar when he too became dictator. Augustus replaced the assassinated Caesar, his legitimacy built on the might of his forces, and only his intelligence and his ceaseless work in favor of his fellow Romans made the pill--the end of the Republic--digestible, this following in the shadow of Caesar who had also worked tirelessly for Rome and its people, a man as loved as he was respected, as would be Augustus. Who could have imagined they would be followed by the likes of Caligula, Nero and Elagabalus, and even Augustus' own choice, his adopted son, the supremely vile Tiberius?

The Curia Julia in the time of Caesar and today.
The Senate gathered in the curia, the word signifying a meeting place. The third Roman king constructed the Curia Hostilia that Sulla later enlarged when he doubled the number of senators from 300 to 600. Destroyed by fire, it was replaced by his son and called the Curia Cornelia. When Caesar tripled the number of senators to 900 he had the curia replaced by the Curia Julia. Caesar was assassinated before its completion, but Augustus finished it, reducing the number of senators to 600 at the same time. The Curia Julia was restored by other emperors, its last restoration terminated in 1937.

With the fall of the kings, the Senate continued on as an advisory group to two Consuls, two in number, perhaps a heritage of the Spartans who elected two kings, one to stay home and govern the city and Spartan lands [ever afraid that their slaves, the helots, would revolt and massacre them all in their sleep], while the second led troops in foreign adventures (3). But these new kings, the Consuls, were limited to a term of a single year, renewable every 10 years only, while the Senate continued on, as said, making it the most important political force in Rome. The Senate passed decrees that were nonbinding, but generally confirmed by the Consuls and obeyed by the people. It was the assembly of the people that originated laws, and if a senatorial decree was in conflict with an assembly law, the law overrode the decree, as senatorial powers were traditional, not binding. But because the Senate sat in continuum and assemblies, like Consuls, came and went, senatorial decrees, although lacking the force of law, became the governing forces of the land. Underlying all this was the fact that the Senate controlled the Roman treasury, the funds that paid the army and salaries. In times of emergencies the Senate could name a dictator, normally for a period of six months, renewable, a man usually chosen from one of the Consuls. [An additional proof of the importance of Consuls was that they too could appoint a dictator, although one Consul could veto the choice of the other, and both could veto the choice of dictator made by the Senate--veto meaning ''I forbid'']. The Senate operated under religious restrictions, could only meet on grounds dedicated to the gods, and only after the auspicious results of sacrifices.

Senate meetings were called by the Consuls at dawn, one of whom gave a speech on the issue under discussion, the issue was then debated by each senator by order of seniority. The final vote could be by show of hands, by voice, or, in important cases, the senators would move to one side of the chamber or the other. The Roman Senate invented the filibuster, literally talking a motion to death. Meetings obligatorily ended at nightfall. The Senate could veto any decision made by a dictator, should they dare do so, their lives, under Sulla, in the balance, but a Tribune could veto any decree passed by the Senate, as stated. The Tribune of the people, or Plebeian Tribune [made up of merchants, craftsmen and farmers], had immense powers under the Republic. It could propose legislation and could veto the actions of the Consuls or the Senate [a fact worth repeating]. Men elected as Tribunes were sacrosanct, meaning that any assault on them was prohibited by law [under the emperors all tribunal powers reverted to the emperor himself, bringing an end to tribunal influence].

Senate membership was controlled by censors, responsible for counting the population of Rome, for public morality [whence our word censorship] and overseeing certain government finances. Early senators had to possess property worth at least one million sesterces [one 2015 estimate placed the value of one sesterce at a ballpark $1.50]. Senators could not engage in banking, commerce or leave Italy without permission. They were also unpaid, but peddled their influence as every magistrate has done since the beginning of time [although senators were not strictly magistrates because they were not voted into office by the people].

Optimates [the best ones] were traditionalists who composed the majority of the Roman Senate, men I'll refer to by the more familiar word patricians. They were opposed to the people and the peoples' popular assemblies and Tribunes, who represented a never-ending threat to Optimate power and finances, a nuisance known under the collective name of Populares, that I'll refer to as plebeians, the common folk, commoners, whom the patricians felt always wanted something, more land and land reform, subsidized grain [and often free grain, as offered by populists like Catiline], the extension of Roman citizenship, *always something.* But as Rome depended more and more on war to ensure its wealth--from the grain and oil that assured Roman survival to the delicate fruits and wondrous tissues that pampered the tastes of the rich-- it depended on its army, made up of plebeians, the reason the Senate was forced to make concessions, especially concerning the senators' Achilles' heel, land reform, which deprived them of wealth, as well as demands for increased citizenship, which diluted their power [citizenship at first granted only to Romans in Rome].

Most men of ambition used the Senate as a tool to expand their power, while others, and not the least [Catiline, Caesar and at one time even Pompey flirted with populism], used the plebeians as today populist politicians find the unorganized and often ill-informed masses easier prey. Patricians were against generals like Caesar and Pompey the Great because their power threatened that of the Senate, whereas they were in favor of Sulla who sought to strip outside assemblies of influence, thusly increasing that of the Senate. Sulla didn't hesitate to massacre large numbers of plebeians, killing an estimated 9,000 Romans, which nonetheless included 1,500 interfering nobles.

The ossified Senate did have its moment of glory when patrician Brutus killed Caesar, senators suddenly becoming *liberators*, republicans who saved the Roman Republic.

As stated, Plebeian officials were called Tribunes, each of whom had two aediles. In time they won the right to become Consuls as well as dictators. They became an integral part of the Senate, and as such the plebeian class drew closer to the patrician class, although patricians could not become plebeians unless adopted by a plebeian. Catiline sought the support of plebeians because it was clear to him that the fastest way to supremacy was through the less well-educated, less well-organized and more-easily manipulated plebes, the major reason he backed land reform, the patricians' nightmare, a plebe's wet dream.

The Senate soon learned how to get around Tribunes. Because they were usually far less well-off than patricians, they could be bribed. They could be promised entry into the Senate, nearly always a Tribune's goal thanks to the greater prestige. In some cases a Tribune could be offered the daughter of a senator, the Tribune's ticket into the good life of property, wealth and luxury, his present enhanced, his future assured. If that failed, there was always murder, as in the case of the Gracchi brothers.

Plebeians reached their ascendancy four times, the first when the Gracchi brothers mobilized the people, in 133 B.C. The brothers, Tiberius and Gaius, were the first to try to institute land reform, land taken from the rich--the foundation of senators' power--and given to the poor who until then had subsisted on handouts. The oldest, Tiberius, wanted to open the ranks of the armies to plebeians by eliminating the need to hold property in order to serve, as had been the case since the early kings. He also favored legislation that would subsidize grain for the poor, as well as free clothing for soldiers who until then had to pay for their own weapons and what they wore. In response, the senators, fearing the confiscation of their lands, sent a force in the Forum that clubbed Tiberius and 300 of his followers to death, the first open bloodshed in 400 years, the reason the Gracchi and their reforms became indelible in the memory of early Romans.

Gaius Gracchus took up the flame years later, increasing the stakes with an additional reform, Roman citizenship to Italians outside the city, Italians who died for Rome and made up 2/3rds of the army, who had been given great autonomy but not citizenship. But an incredible event occurred: Senators rose up against him, which was expected, but this time the senators were backed by the very people Tiberius and Gaius had spent their lives fighting for, Rome's underclass, the poor. Poor Romans who feared they would lose status and perks such as subsidized grain, and be submerged by "foreign" Italians who would take the best seats at the games and festivals and who, due to their numbers, would leave the poor with smaller bribes during elections. This time the Senate didn't need to intervene. Roman mobs did the work for them, and while three thousand Gracchi supporters were slaughtered, Gaius committed suicide, falling on his sword. The brothers' reforms were abandoned, except for the subsidized distribution of grain. Classicist J. C. Stobart states that the Gracchi were naïve victims, "deaf to the baser instincts of human nature".

Tiberius and Gaius Gracchus

The second time the plebeians seized power was under Gaius Marius and his son, who held Rome from 87 to 82 B.C. It started in 88 B.C. when Rome sent an army to rein in King Mithridates of Pontus, but it was defeated on the battlefield. Sulla was dispatched to repair the damage and while he was away Gaius Marius, a Tribune, revoked his command, proof of the tremendous powers the plebeians had acquired. Sulla returned to Rome and massacred the followers of Marius who were not quick enough to escape the city, as had Marius. Sulla then sailed to Pontus where he made peace with Mithridates. During this second absence Marius returned to Rome where he ruled with an absolute disregard for Roman law. Sulla returned to the city in 83 B.C. and slaughtered Marius' followers, sparring a certain 17-

year-old, Julius Caesar, as recounted in the chapter on Caesar. Sulla was made dictator, meaning only someone selected to stabilize the government. Among his first moves was the strengthening of the Senate, which immediately passed legislation reducing the powers of the plebeian Tribune, depriving it of its capacity to veto decrees issued by the Senate, which reduced the Tribune to quasi uselessness. [Later, however, the boy Sulla had spared, Julius Caesar, reestablished many of the Tribune's prerogatives, although Caesar waited until Sulla was safely underground. Some 28 years following this, Caesar, Sulla's attentive student, marched on Rome and made himself dictator, all due to the precedent set by Sulla.] Sulla transferred control of the courts to the Senate and, in order to prevent a man from seizing power as he himself had done, he passed a law stipulating that Consuls be sent abroad after serving their consular year in Rome, and not be allowed a second consulship before the lapse of 10 years, which was, in reality, an affirmation of a law already in existence. As for Marius, he served a total of seven consulships, the most in Roman history, and died--his conscience apparently untroubled by the thousands who had died during his revolts--in his bed, at the very ripe old age of 71. It was Marius, by the way, as both a statesman and a general, who organized the legions [the word means levy] into cohorts, dividing legions of about 5,000 men into 10 cohorts. There were six centurions per cohort, and within each cohort were tents of eight men who became tighter than brothers. What a soldier most desired, wrote Plutarch, ''was the sight of his commanding officer openly eating the same bread as him, or lying on a plain straw mattress, or lending a hand to dig a ditch or raise a palisade. What they admire in a leader is the willingness to share the danger and the hardship, rather than the ability to win them honor and wealth, and they are more fond of officers who are prepared to make efforts alongside them than they are of those who let them take things easy'' [a quotation found in Adrian Goldsworthy's *In the Name of Rome*]. This was the secret of the success of Sulla, Pompey, Caesar and Gaius Marius.

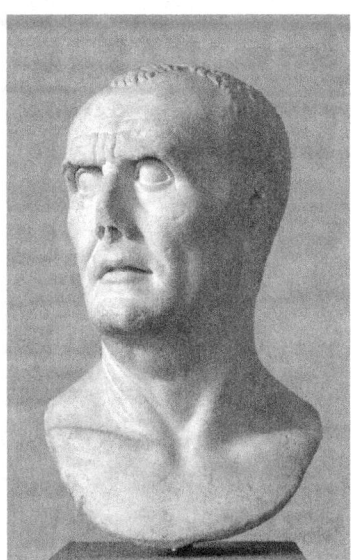

Gaius Marius

To this Sallust adds that soldering was the true school of life, where men competed for honors, their victories the source of repute, nobility and wealth, but more importantly a way of bringing honor to themselves in the eyes of their comrades, in the tradition of the Spartans (3) and Sacred Band of Thebes (6) who, when caught by the enemy, requested they be killed with a sword blow to the chest and not the back, so as not to bring dishonor on themselves when found by their lovers. Roman soldiers were eight to a tent, and no god in existence had more importance to the eyes of a man than did his seven tent mates. The delight of young men were weapons, armor and his horse maintained Sallust, far more so than ''loose women or the pleasures of the table.''

Like Cicero and Emperor Hadrian, Marius was new to Rome, a ''new man'', *novus homo*, men who had to work infinitely harder because they were born without ancient roots and wealth [or, at least, not lucky enough to have been born in Rome]. The genius of Marius was recruiting an army from the poor and forming legions represented by a silver eagle. Men soon formed bonds that were tighter than those between family members, their comrades in arms they would unhesitatingly die for, and if an eagle were lost during a battle, it was invariably because all the men had been massacred. The whole nation mourned them, and emperors sent out new armies to retrieve the eagles. This tradition began with Marius. Before, men supplied their own weapons; now, thanks to Marius, they received leather protection, swords [the *gladius*] and daggers [the *pugio*] for close-contract fighting. Gradually, the army evolved from serving between harvests and plantings to lifelong engagement, up to 22 years. Conscription was initiated when enough volunteers could no longer be found, but it was limited to 16 years, for boys 17 or older. [It was at age 17 that Catiline entered the Social War, a war between Roman citizens and surrounding Italian entities that fought for Rome and paid heavy Roman taxes, but were denied Roman citizenship. Catiline served with distinction and those Italian allies who had not joined the rebellion were given citizenship in a law passed by Lucius Julius Caesar, the consular cousin of a certain Julius Caesar.]

Marius had held more consulships than any man before him [proof that a waiting period of 10 years between censorships was far from being ironclad]. As a teenager Marius had found an eagle's nest with seven eggs, an extreme rarity because eagles usually produced three. Because eagles were sacred to Jupiter, he knew that the number seven would be decisive in his life. He was popular among his soldiers and gained their loyalty by eating and working side by side with them. Marius [157 – 86 B.C.] at first gained the love of a certain segment of the population by opening the army to everyone, regardless of class, thusly giving employment to thousands of poor, providing them with retirement and health benefits, and new recruits were no longer required to possess property, a seismic change in Roman tradition. He also saved Rome from descending Teutonic hordes, winning a great deal of thanks at the outset, but once he possessed power, wrote Plutarch, he not only put to death anyone suspected of not favoring him, he would have a man slaughtered on the street if he deemed his greeting not sufficiently obsequious. Marius was the first man responsible for the destruction of the Republic when he opened up the army to all citizens, and then promised them land at the end of their service, a policy later shared by Sulla and Caesar, thanks to which soldiers became loyal *to generals only*, not senators who tried by every means to keep property for themselves, their source of power, prestige and wealth.

The third moment of plebeian glory was when Caesar was elected consul in 59 B.C. and formed the First Triumvirate [see Caesar's chapter] alongside Pompey the Great and Marcus Crassus, Rome's wealthiest citizen. Here too it was a question of land reform, land Caesar and Pompey, both generals, wished turned over to their veterans, ensuring the eternal thanks and support of the army, soon to become the true power of Rome. This was the first agrarian reform since the Gracchi in 133 B.C. The fourth and last triumph of the plebeians was again under Caesar, himself a Populares [along with Mark Antony who owed his influence, as well as a Consulship, directly to Caesar], despite his aristocratic [Optimate] roots. Pompey too was a popularist, certainly influenced by his deep love for the men he led into battle, but later in life he drifted towards the Optimates.

Plebeians were open to populists like Catiline and Caesar because after making huge political and agrarian advances their power began to steadily diminish. It was the plebeians who fought the wars against Hannibal, leaving their farms to fall into disrepair, and when they returned home their accumulated debts obliged them to sell their lands to the already landed patricians. During their absence the wealth of the patricians had increased due to the higher prices they could demand for goods during wartime shortages, and also thanks to the cost of labor which decreased due to the huge influx of slaves brought into Rome by Roman conquests. And with the fall of Carthage, new commercial routes opened up, and only the patricians had the funds necessary to build the ships they manned with ever-cheaper slaves.

The ultimate power in Rome was called *imperium*, the power to command, a power held by Consuls, Tribunes [as well as their assistants, the aediles] and dictators. The first kings of Rome held *imperium*, their bodies sacrosanct. Dictators were above senators and the Tribunes. After the death of Caesar, and the establishment of the Roman Empire under Augustus, both the Senate and the Tribunes lost their eminence.

Born Gaius Octavius Thurinus.
His regnal name: Imperator Caesar Divi Filius Augustus.
The principle subjects of this book lived in a time known as the Roman Republic. The Republic ended with the death of Caesar and the assumption of Octavian, given the title of Augustus by the Senate, a man who lived for the people and was so beloved by them that he was able to usher in reforms, a reorganization and evolution of the Constitution that changed the Roman Republic into the Roman Empire. There is no other person in the history of the world to be compared to Augustus, in wisdom he was Solon, in his devolution to Rome and Romans he was an Erasmus. He was saintly in his mores, and when he felt his time had come, after exiling his daughter Julia to the island of Pandateria and ordering the death of his grandson Postumus, on captivity on another island, Planasia, he ate the figs he himself raised in his garden, the only delicacy supported by his dissident stomach, perhaps in the knowledge that they'd been poisoned by his beloved wife Livia, whose son Tiberius would be the first of a string of emperors as dastardly as any known to the ancient world.

PART V

CATILINE AND CAESAR
CATO AND MARK ANTONY
CICERO
CRASSUS AND POMPEY

AUGUSTUS

The company in which Catiline found himself when he enlisted in 90 B.C. contained some men of immense influence, one of whom was Rome's first dictator, largely forgotten but of huge significance, Sulla, another known to every school child, Pompey the Great, and a third, greater than both combined, Julius Caesar. We've covered the life and times of Sulla, so now let's look into that of Caesar and Pompey.

The most accurate image concerning the sexual side of Caesar was that when he saw a woman or a man who aroused him, he would go into the nearest room and have the object of his lust paged by a servant. He then adjusted his robes which, like everything he did, were different from his contemporaries in that the sleeves were long and the robe was taken in at the waist, leading Sulla to say of him, before the Senate, beware of that belt-girded boy. He was sexually insatiable. After momentarily appeasing his libido he would return to his seat, again tuned into the business at hand, exactly as a dog would copulate and then run off to other concerns, its tail wagging innocently until coming across the next temptation. Catullus accused him of having intercourse with Mamurra, whom Catullus nicknamed Rod. He stated they both suffered from venereal disease, Caesar's picked up in Rome, Mamurra's in his hometown of Formiae. "Both are equally debauched, like twins, both learned scholars in affairs of the bed, both friendly rivals in pursuit of girls, both lewd lechers." When Catullus later apologized to Caesar he was invited to dinner, his apology accepted.

Caesar's life was extremely satisfying because he had the power to assuage his lust whenever and with whomever he wished, and often, very often. His partner for a moment was rarely required more than once, and she was most likely married, perhaps because he relished the risk. Perhaps too Caesar found married women more experienced, capable of those small things that can bring a man pleasantly up and over. Or perhaps, too, he knew that she would keep her mouth shut, that she would never hound him--if she wished to go on living. So sexually he took full advantage of life and his body, giving of himself while taking in equal measure, the veritable *raison d'être* of our existence.

His chief mistress was Servilia, whom he had known for so many years that many believed she was the mother of Brutus, his future murderer, although Caesar would have been 15 at the time, certainly not an impossibility [but still seriously doubted by most authorities, despite rumors at the time that this was so]. One of Servilia's daughters married Cassius, another of Caesar's future assassins, and Servilia was the half-sister of Cato, whose wife Caesar was bedding [among so many, many others, for Caesar appreciated married women, as reported, silent so not to be executed by their husbands, who had the right to do so if they were caught in *fragrante delicto*]. She is said to have offered another of her daughters to Caesar when his interest in her waned, while some historians claim the daughter in question was Caesar's own. During Caesar's war against Pompey he saved Brutus, who was on Pompey's side [despite the fact that it was Pompey who had killed Brutus' father].

Just a word about Cato. Cato [Marcus Porcius Cato Uticensis] was Rome's conscience, known for his integrity and refusal of corruption. Cato was a Republican who, at age 14, hearing of the murders carried out by Sulla, asked his tutor for a sword in order to kill the dictator himself, his intent so strong that the tutor wouldn't let him out of his sight. Hugely admired for his rhetorical style, Cato was, philosophically, a Stoic. Stoicism, named after *stoa*, the Greek colonnades that surrounded the Agora in Athens. Since the cosmos ruled the fates of men, and men would be eternally too unknowledgeable to understand the cosmos, one had to accept one's fate willingly, believed Stoics, whatever it was. This acceptance applied to death which a man had to face in a manly manner, seeing that forfeiting one's life was only giving back what henceforth belonged to another.

He fought in the war against Spartacus, described in the chapter on Pompey. Although rich, he lived like a Stoic pauper, spending lavishly only on the burial of the brother he adored. Like Cicero, he made a point of showing himself scrupulously honest in his administrative and senatorial duties, never bending, as Cicero often did, to the demands of politicians like Pompey and Caesar.

He voted, as did Cicero, for the execution of Catiline's supporters, accused of plotting the murder of Consuls and magistrates, this against Caesar who felt they should be imprisoned, not put to death. The executions envisioned by Cicero and Cato would take place without trials, setting a dangerous precedent, felt Caesar, and he was right. During the death-penalty discussion on the Senate floor, a message was transferred to Caesar. Seeing it, Cato proclaimed that it was from Catiline followers, an attempt to corrupt Caesar. A man of incredible self-control, Caesar could have read out the message before the full Senate. Instead, he passed it on to Cato, who turned red while reading it. It was a billet-doux from Cato's half-sister, Caesar favored mistress Servilia. Cato proclaimed that Caesar was a "drunken fool", which brought laughter because all knew that Caesar rarely drank even wine, while Cato was a notorious lush.

Later, in another debate before the Senate, Caesar tried to put through agrarian land reform that would provide land for his troops on their retirement, the chief way a general could assure himself of their unfailing loyalty. Because the lands were public and brought in $1/4^{th}$ of the Republic's income, Cato decided to filibuster it by talking until nightfall. To prevent him from doing so, Caesar, at the time a Consul, sent his bodyguards, his lictors, to bodily remove Cato from the building.

It was Cato's opposition to Caesar that forced Caesar to cross the Rubicon and take possession of both Rome and the Senate, a carbon-copy of what Sulla had done. This provoked a Civil War with Pompey, defeated in the Battle of Pharsalus [48 B.C.]. Later, Caesar defeated an army led by Cato [the Battle of Thapsus--46 B.C.], after a sojourn with a certain Cleopatra whom he placed on the throne of Egypt.

Unwilling to live under Caesar, Cato committed suicide by stabbing himself in the stomach, wonderfully told by Plutarch: "Cato did not immediately die of the wound, but struggling, fell off the bed, and throwing down a little mathematical table that stood by, made such a noise that the servants, hearing it, cried out. And immediately his son and all his friends came into the chamber, where, seeing him lie weltering in his own blood, great part of his bowels out of his body, but himself still alive and able to look at them, they all stood in horror. The physician went to him and would have put in his bowels, which were not pierced, and sewed up the wound, had Cato not recovered and, understanding the intention, thrust away the physician, plucked out his own bowels and, tearing open the wound, immediately expired.''

It was Cato who had proclaimed before the Punic Wars, at each session of the Senate, ''Carthage must be destroyed'', which led to the massacre of thousands, including children, the survivors sold into slavery, the reader free to judge Cato in his entirety after further reading on the life of this unique human being [see Sources].

Cato.
Cato was universally described as upright, austere, firm, the scourge of the wicked, restrained, strictly honest, fanatically devoted to seeing justice done, a man who possessed a noble soul, one who divorced his wife for unseemly behavior. His son was killed at the Battle of Philippe and his daughter married Caesar's assassin, Brutus.

Caesar appreciated men. ''When sent to raise a fleet in Bithynia Caesar wasted so much time at King Nicomedes' court that a sexual relationship between them was suspected, and even when he left the king to regain his headquarters, he dashed back at the first opportunity," writes Suetonius. In the Senate, when stating that he would destroy his opponents, someone cried out, "A feat difficult for a woman," implying that the woman in question was he. Caesar retorted, "And why not? The Amazons once ruled over vast areas of Asia." Suetonius tells us that Licinius Calvus published this verse:

> The riches of Bithynia's king
> Whom Caesar on his couch amused.

Marcus Bibulus called him "The Queen of Bithynia who slept with the monarch and now wants to become one." Octavius, when presented to Pompey and Caesar, called the first King and the second Queen. Roman guests at one of Nicomedes' banquets stated, shocked, that Caesar had served as his cup bearer, exactly as Ganymede was Zeus' [although Caesar was there as an ambassador representing Rome]. Suetonius tells us that his own soldiers sang about how Caesar had conquered the Gauls, but Nicomedes had conquered Caesar [similar to what Diogenes of Sinope said about Alexander the Great who had been vanquished but once, by the thighs of his lover Hephaestion]. Cicero, in a letter, wrote: "Caesar was led to Nicomedes' bedchamber where, spread out on the king's couch, he lost his virginity." And once, in the Senate, when Caesar mentioned how much Nicomedes had done for Rome, Cicero exclaimed, "Enough! We know what he gave you and what you gave him in return." Caesar didn't kill Cicero but his friend Mark Antony avenged him by having Cicero's head lopped off. And finally the immortal sentence handed down by Curio, saying Caesar was "every woman's husband and every man's wife."

Caesar, impeccable manners, aristocratic poise.

Marcus Brutus felt that Caesar's death would save the Republic, the reason he and others assassinated him. At the Battle of Philippi Brutus committed suicide and the Roman world was divided between Octavian and Mark Antony for a decade, before Antony and his political paramour Cleopatra committed suicide in their turn, leaving Octavian, now Augustus, to transform Rome's cherished institutions into the Roman Empire. As for Brutus, his ashes were sent to his mother from the battlefield, after which Brutus' wife purportedly killed herself by swallowing hot coals.

Caesar was said to have descended from Aeneas himself. He lost his father young, as Alcibiades had lost his, and like the extremely versatile Greek, Caesar had grown up surrounded by men who spoke of laws and government, men who excelled in oratory, many of them the finest speakers in one of the world's most beautiful languages, a language in which one could express oneself in gorgeous verse and, as in the army, the crudest possible idiom. Schooled by the finest tutors, often slaves [who made up from 1/3rd to half of the Roman population], introduced to literature and books in his father's and his father's friends' libraries, from childhood he was put on the path to great achievement. As the poet wrote, given his background, ''What did Caesar have better to do than to rule the world?'' He ran, he swam in the Tiber, he worked out in the gymnasia, not naked as did the Greeks, and not the prey of sexual predators, or at least none that too overtly made their lust known, unlike the gymnasia of the Greeks. He learned to handle weapons, swords and spears, and was an excellent rider, maneuvering a horse with the pressure of his knees. From his statues we see him as being slight of build, well-proportioned and handsome.

All periods of time were harrowing for the Romans who gained wealth through wars and new lands through conquest. Caesar's own childhood was marked by the Social Wars: While the inhabitants of Rome were Roman citizens, the inhabitants of other cities in Italy, outside of Rome, were not. They had to content themselves with furnishing Rome with money and troops, while having no say in government and the other benefits offered Roman citizens. One senator, Livius Drusus, finding this state of affairs unjust, tried to convince the Senate to offer Italians, who fought and died for Rome, citizenship. For his troubles he was assassinated, providing the spark that provoked the Italian city-states to revolt. They banded together to form an entity they called Italia, with a new capital, Italica [nearly 2000 years before Garibaldi!]. As the revolutionaries were former Roman soldiers, they were extremely battle hardened and numbered 100,000. The Senate had a change of heart and citizenship in one form or another was offered to Italian cities, but only up to the Po River.

Catiline took part in the Social Wars, a boy of 20, soldiering under Sulla, 50. As a young student of war, he kept close watch over Sulla's career and advancement, especially the years to come when Sulla occupied Rome with his troops, using proscription to put thousands to death, proscriptions that allowed him to take their property and wealth, making Sulla himself fabulously rich, although most historians doubt that this was his aim in life, unlike Catiline's enemies who claimed that Sulla's seizures of other men's fortunes was the main motivation for Catiline's conspiracies.

At age 15 Caesar exchanged the *toga praetexta* with its purple fringe for the pure white *toga virilis*. He was now a recognized citizen of Rome, responsible, in case of his father's death, for his mother and sisters and younger brothers. In Caesar's case, he had become the paterfamilias. He also put aside his *bulla praetexta*, a charm of gold held in a leather sack that parents put around their boy's neck, at age 9 days [time to see if he lived through the unsanitary conditions of childbirth], aimed at warding off evil spirits. The bulla, along with a lock of the boy's hair or, if the boy could, the first shavings from his chin, were placed on the family altar and dedicated to the Lares, guardian deities of the household. Mothers recuperated the bulla to protect the boy as he grew, to protect him especially from envious people who might wish him harm. The ceremony of the Lares must have been very moving and certainly would be today if it existed [in its place some nations cut off a boy's prepuce, disfiguring him for life, depriving him of what should be his own choice when he reaches the age of reason]. The ceremony took place on the 17th of March. Forty-four years later, nearly to the day, he would be assassinated by men who had worshipped him until then, one of whom could have *conceivably* been his son, as Brutus was born when Caesar was nearly 16, and Brutus' mother was a very long-term mistress of Caesar's, as mentioned earlier.

At age 16 he married Cornelia. An extremely telling story about Caesar's courage is that Sulla, who didn't shy away from killing 1,500 nobles and 9,000 young men on a parade ground, each begging for his precious life, ordered Caesar to rid himself of Cornelia in favor of someone from Sulla's own family. Sulla had already ordered the Great Pompey to do likewise and Pompey, despite the fact that his wife was fully pregnant, had done so. But Caesar refused, the only man in Rome to show such immensurable courage.

At age 19 he was sent as an ambassador to King Nicomedes IV's court in search of warships, but where, as reported, he dallied a rather long time. Adrian Goldsworthy states that he may have been dazzled by the Hellenic culture that reigned in the East, so different from crude Rome. Goldsworthy adds, ''Perhaps the nineteen-year-old did feel and succumb to an attraction to an older man--'experimenting with his sexuality' would probably be the fashionable modern euphemism.'' The reality was far more prosaic, I would imagine. In Rome men just had sex, often with whatever was closest at hand, be it a boy or a girl. Male-male sexuality, although not nearly as open and accepted as in Greece, was nonetheless the norm for *every* boy and man. Of course, an ambassador shacking up with a king while on an official mission was not a situation known to your everyday Roman citizen.

Both Nicomedes and Bithynia deserve a word. Bithynia encircled today's Istanbul, making it a vital crossroads between Turkey and Greece, a fertile land with superb ports and endless trade. It was Hellenized by Thracians and occupied later by Persians. The Bithynians knew how to take advantage of their forests and mountains to remain free, which they did even when attacked by Alexander the Great. The constant attacks by Mithridates [covered in the life of Sulla] forced Bithynia to seek accommodations with Rome. Nicomedes sought close ties with Rome, very close concerning his friendship with Caesar, but nonetheless so close that at his death Nicomedes bequeathed his kingdom to Rome!

At age 25 Caesar was captured by pirates while sailing the Aegean, a plague against commerce that Pompey would later take care of. Caesar's reaction is reported as being gutsy, telling the pirates to request a ransom of 50 talents when they had originally requested 20 [he felt he was worth more than just 20], ordering them to shut up when he took a nap or slept at night. He read them poetry, led them in calisthenics, playfully warning them that he would have their heads once he was freed. The pirates supposedly grew found of him and wished him well when his shipmates returned with the money for his liberation. Caesar returned with a small army of his own and crucified them all, after first slitting their throats--saving them from atrocious suffering, in thanks for their comradeship.

Back in Rome he was named to a series of offices--Tribune, quaestor, Pontifex Maximus, praetor and others that I won't go into as they do not advance our story and, anyway, they will all lose their importance in a few short years with the coming of the greatest of all emperors, Augustus.

From Rome Caesar was sent to squelch rebellions in Gaul. And from Gaul he went to the Rubicon.

In crossing the Rubicon, Caesar is said to have borrowed the Greek playwright Menander's words, "let the die be cast," leaving no doubt that he knew his act would trigger civil war. Since the cruelty of Sulla, the very thought of civil war, for Romans, was synonymous with annihilation, and the fact that Sulla died peacefully in his bed made clear the inexistence of justice. That so many men followed Caesar in such an apparently insane venture is proof of the incredible bond he was able to forge between them and himself, a far from easy task involving rough men little known for their patience and empathy. Yet Caesar had constantly awarded them, sharing the riches brought forth from his victories. This was not true in Rome where the people cared little for him, and where problems arising between Caesar and Pompey were the affairs of the nobility, concerning the people not at all. They just wanted to live reasonably well, raise their families in peace and die in bed, living on immortally through their sons.

In 50 B.C., at the age of 50, Caesar had been requested to disband his troops in Gaul--where his victories had placed him in the firmament of Roman heroes, just behind the Great Pompey himself--and return home. Gaul had provided Caesar and his men, alone with glory, with immeasurable wealth through plunder and the number of slaves they had amassed. But Caesar hesitated to return to Rome, fearing that he would be prosecuted for a number of events that had taken place in previous years. He had become Consul in 59 B.C., after one of the most contested elections in Roman history, where bribery was beyond all limits. He formed an alliance with super-rich Crassus and super-powerful Pompey, even marrying Pompey's daughter, Julia. The three, united, were able to pass a number of bills, one of which provided land for legionnaires, a soldier's wet dream come true. Caesar had been elected Consul with Marcus Bibulus who was against the bill. In response Caesar had the poor retch splattered with excrement. With power had come jealousies and new enemies, all of which were now out to get him, even Pompey. The poet Lucan would later add, "Caesar could not accept a superior, and Pompey could not accept an equal." So Caesar came up with the plan to return to Rome accompanied by his legions, and since an army was forbidden to enter the city, he would remain outside until elected Consul, after which he would become inviolable, totally untouchable by those out to get him. His plan was not without precedent, as both Pompey and Crassus had done the same thing in 71 B.C.

Pompey had infinitely more men and money than Caesar. He even boasted that he had only to stamp his feet on the ground for soldiers to spring from the soil, as the great Achilles had done to encourage ants to leave their tunnels, immediately changed into Myrmidons by the sun. But Pompey needed time to get both men and wealth together. This, Caesar didn't accord him, proof of his knowledge of events and his military sense. Taken off guard, Pompey fled Rome for Brindisi where he embarked for Greece. Caesar left Rome in the hands of Mark Antony.

At first blush, this seemed a strange choice. Antony's father, Marcus Antonius, had been an incompetent and corrupt lush who had been given power, says Cicero, because by bribing him one could obtain whatever one wished. Marcus [the father] fancied himself a Sulla and behaved with such extravagance [bacchanals and drinking bouts] that he attracted the never-complacent eye of Cicero whom he tried to assassinate as a first step to seizing power in Rome [it was actually reported that he wished to burn down the city]. As the Romans were afraid of what he might do next, he was murdered, with the approbation of Cicero. This most probably entered into Mark Antony's decision, later, to put Cicero to death, although Cicero's hatred and vile words concerning Antony would have been more than enough; not only did Antony want Cicero's head, but he also had his hands cut off and sent to him, the hands that had written such vile filth. Antony would have had to have been a saint not to have been influenced by his dad, and the one thing we know for certain about Antony is that he was in no way a saint. Antony was said to have borrowed a huge amount of money from his lover Gaius Scribonius Curio who was deathly afraid of his father finding out. The claim was made by Cicero who was a close friend of Curio's, a claim both to the debt and to Antony's being Curio's lover; and, again, as a close friend, Cicero should therefore have known if they were frolicking in the hay. In fact, Cicero claimed that Antony had many male lovers from whom he extracted large sums, as he had from Curio. Curio, Antony and their companions soon became notorious in Rome, as Alcibiades had been in Athens, for their reckless, drunken behavior, and as was also true with Alcibiades, their families were too well known and too wealthy for Romans to be able to curb their mindless turbulence. Antony eventually became a staff officer in Caesar's armies in Gaul and they became fast friends. Thanks to Gallic plunder, Caesar is said to have loaned great sums of money to Romans for political gain, among whom was Curio whose debts Caesar paid off to the tune of millions.

Mark Antony.

Upon the death of Caesar, Antony and Octavian entered into a double dictatorship. In dire need of funds, they met on an island, each surrounded by 300 men at close range, 5,000 on each bank of the river, one man searching the other for hidden daggers before dressing a list of the hundreds of men they would kill as payment for their opposition, but especially in order to raise money, about whom historian Appian wrote, ''The point was reached where a person was murdered because he had a town house or country estate.'' Cicero was on the list, who had accused Antony, to his face, of being ''a common rent-boy who charged a fee, and a steep one at that. You were as wedded to Curio as if he'd given you a wedding dress.'' Cicero's severed head, his tongue pulled out and pierced with a long pin, was delivered to Antony, as well as the hand that had written filth about the new Roman dictator.

Later, following the death of Pompey, Caesar would have to relieve Antony of his functions when he stole Pompey's property, after maintaining that he had bought it. Still later, Antony would hear of the planned assassination of Caesar and try to warn him, but too late.

From his youth onwards Antony was a good general, a loyal friend to Caesar, but little else: a gambler, a rent-boy always in deepest debt, a ceaseless womanizer, the lunkhead who killed Cicero.

Cicero.

A man who needed stability but was born in an age of change, a conservative in a time of revolution, a man who sang his own praises, who loved no one but his daughter and the young male friends he frequented, apparently platonically, a man about whom the historian Aufidius Bassus wrote, ''A day did not pass when it was in someone's interest to see him dead.'' Cicero's son posted the announcement of Antony's suicide on the exact place in the Forum where Antony had displayed his father's head and hand. ''In this way Heaven entrusted to the family of Cicero the final punishment of Antony,'' wrote Plutarch.

Before racing to Brindisi to stop Pompey from sailing away from Italy, Caesar made a stopover in Rome where he assured every one of his good intentions, promised the people that they would not lack for wheat, and awarded each citizen 300 sesterces, a sum easy to raise as he broke into the treasury--literally axing down the door--and made off with 15,000 gold bars, 30,000 silver bars and 30,000,000 sesterces. Leaving Mark Antony in charge of the city, he finally set off for Brindisi but arrived too late to stop Pompey from sailing to Greece. He too embarked for Greece and met up with Pompey and his troops at Dyrrhachium.

Pompey must have been a truly extraordinary man judging from the caliber of those who respected and followed him, beginning with Cicero who was no man's fool. He was also followed by Brutus, whose father Pompey had nonetheless murdered because he had rebelled against his growing authority. Remember that during the wars against Mithridates Pompey had gained the sobriquet "teenage butcher", but he had been wise enough to back Sulla, thereby saving his head. Pompey's father had been a noble and a general, known for his greed, greed that was transformed into the wealth that Pompey inherited. As a general Pompey secured Sicily, guaranteeing Rome's supply of wheat. There followed other victories in Africa, thanks to which Sulla hailed Pompey as *Magnus*, the Great. Crassus, the wealthiest man in Italy, was given the task of bringing an end to the revolt led by Spartacus. He did so, lining the Appian Way with their crucified bodies, 6,000. But Pompey, returning to Rome, came upon the remnant of Spartacus' army and captured 5,000 that he led to Rome, thereby winning credit for ending the revolt. [The body of Spartacus, who was thought to have been killed by Crassus' legions, was never found.]

Crassus.

Crassus was the richest man in Rome according to most authorities, second to Pompey stated others. His relations with Caesar were bad, in part because Caesar bedded his wife, and they were bad with Pompey whom Crassus found too flamboyant, Pompey who, during a Triumph, dressed 10,000 tables laden with food and wine, and offered three months of free grain to each citizen. It was Crassus who ended the Slave Wars, but Pompey who got the credit because Pompey's captives were herded into Rome, while Crassus' captives were crucified, their bodies mostly unseen because they were stretched out over miles along the Via Appia. While Crassus was unfailingly loyal and trustworthy towards friends, Pompey moved with the tide, even giving up his wife and marrying one of Sulla's daughters when Sulla ordered him to do so. Pompey was called a teenage butcher who apparently took pleasure in murdering senators, yet was given the name *magnus* by the people, while behind the scenes it was Crassus who filled the veritable needs of Romans.

Adrian Goldsworthy writes that Crassus, whose business activities spanned from Rome to the provinces, bought up property at fire-sale prices when buildings caught fire, and then sent in his own fire brigade, the world's first, to put them out. Goldsworthy goes on to related the wonderful story of the Vestal Virgin whom Crassus was bedding, the price for which, if she were found guilty, was her entombment, alive. But Crassus said he frequented her only because he wished to buy her house, and as this was what he did for a living, both he and she were believed. When the Vestal Virgin was freed, Crassus ordered her to *really* sell the house to him, and because she wished to go on breathing, she did.

As piracy had become the plague of the Mediterranean, Pompey was called on to end it, a task no one else had been able to accomplish. With a genius for organization, he divided up the area into thirteen zones and sent out a general and a fleet to comb through every nook and corner of the western Mediterranean, bringing piracy to an end in just forty days. [Although some modern observers think that he accomplished far more by bribing the pirates than by really fighting them, and as his victory had taken place with such incredible rapidity, this is not difficult to believe.] Freeing the seas from pirates meant opening them to trade and the assurance that Rome would not lack for food and rich imports, all of which made Pompey wildly popular. He went on to Jerusalem where he discovered vast riches in the Jewish temple, and, against all expectations, he left everything intact. Thanks to such clemency, when he again returned to Rome it was with the entire East in his pocket. The Greeks acknowledged him as a god, something that cost them little but had the potential of reaping great rewards in goodwill and trade. He rode through the streets of his native city triumphantly, with a servant murmuring in his ear, ''Remember, you are a man, not a god.'' Plutarch stated that Pompey's achievements outshone even those of Alexander the Great.

That was Pompey, that was his glory, until he embarked for Greece, followed by Caesar right up to the gates of the city of Dyrrhachium. Along the way there had been problems. Some of the ships carrying Caesar's men from Brindisi to Greece had been waylaid by Pompey's navy and captured. Both ships and men were deliberately torched. The Ninth Legion revolted because of Caesar's decision to be clement to the towns Caesar went through in both Italy and Greece, deciding, for example, to not burn Brindisi to the ground for helping Pompey escape. This clemency deprived the troops of spoils, an integral part of their pay. Caesar decided to apply the traditional punishment, decimation, recounts Appian. One man out of every ten would be beaten to death by his fellow soldiers. When the men begged for forgiveness, Caesar order 120 of the ringleaders brought before him. Decimation would apply to them only, meaning 12 would perish. Luckily, before the sentence was carried forth Caesar discovered that one of the 12 hadn't even been in camp when the revolt broke out. He had been chosen by a commander who simply wanted to get rid of him. The commander in question took his place. From then on, the Ninth was the most valorous of all of Caesar's legions.

Pompey.
Pompey was known for his virile lovemaking, leaving his women with scratch marks as well as, claimed his mistress Flora, toothmarks. Generous to a fault, he would give his favorite courtesan to a friend should the friend request her. Courtesans were often well-educated, witty and charming, they could dance and sing and had a doctorate in how to bring a man most pleasurably up and over.

Marriages were for gaining status by entering into a better family, for wealth through a woman's holdings and dowry, and for the production of sons, a man's only assurance of immortality.

At Dyrrhachium Caesar blocked Pompey's troops inside the city. Pompey refused battle because it was winter and he felt he could starve Caesar's legions into giving up the siege. As Dyrrhachium was on the coast of Albania [Durrës today] and given the fact that Pompey had a quasi-unlimited supply of ships, he could be easily provisioned. But Caesar's men were motivated, stating that they would eat the bark off trees in necessary. His troops were nonetheless confronted by two major problems: the first was the battlefield scourge, diarrhea, humiliating and dehumanizing; the second was an order given by Pompey to shot arrows into the hundreds of campfires, thousands of them, a hit-and-miss attempt to kill Caesar's men, one that worked until the men moved away to sleep in the cold. Finally Caesar gave up and withdrew.

It was said that many of Pompey's men, heartened by the withdrawal of Caesar, sent representatives to Rome to buy up land and houses that would serve as the foundation of their future wealth, as at that moment prices were garage-sale low due to the pessimism concerning the outcome of the war. But such optimism was not the case for Pompey. In fact, Cicero says that after Dyrrhachium Pompey "ceased being a general".

Their next encounter was at Pharsalus, a battle in which Pompey was reported to have lost 6,000 men to Caesar's 200, although 20 centurions died, the cream of each legion, each responsible for 1,000 men under their orders. As the centurions were the vanguard of the troops, they were also by far the best paid and the first to die. Brutus, the son of Caesar's mistress, Servilia, [whom many historians believe to have been *his* son] was captured but spared. In fact, Caesar sent a party out looking for him. Pompey escaped. The other inhabitants of Pharsalus didn't fare as well. His soldiers, furious at having been defeated at Dyrrhachium, took out their anger on the population and Caesar, usually so moderate, gave them their head. Those within the town who did not commit suicide were raped and slaughtered. The next morning the soldiers walked or rode away, their stomachs full of food and drink, their heads cleared and their balls empty for the first time in months. Left behind were men and boys sprawled out in the distorted forms of rigor mortis, their bodies pierced, sliced or dismembered by dagger and sword. Their women folk were spread out too, but they were on their backs naked, their legs push up and thighs open, frozen in the postures that death found them, some knifed while still penetrated by men inured or even aroused by their suffering, achieving release while seeking traction in the brew of blood and semen at their feet. The silence of their leave-taking, after a night of screams, was deafening.

Pompey sailed to Egypt where the young king, Cleopatra's brother and husband, had him beheaded the moment his feet touched the beach of Alexandria.

So ended the life of this extraordinary man, harbinger of Caesar's own death just four years in the future.

Caesar had the leader of Ptolemy's army and Ptolemy's regent, a eunuch, put to the sword. Plutarch says that the body of

Pompey was cremated by Pompey's freed slave, using planks from a rotting fishing boat. Caesar had the ashes sent to his wife for burial, and his head interred at Alexandria. Ptolemy, in an attempt to flee, drowned in the Nile.

Those of us born on the planet Earth know about the ups and downs of Caesar's relationship with Cleopatra, which will therefore be bypassed here. Even if he had married her, a marriage was recognized only between Roman citizens. Their association lasted fourteen years and a boy was born, Caesarion. Cleopatra is thought to have visited Rome several times.

Caesar named his grandnephew, Gaius Octavius, the future Augustus, as his adopted son and heir, stating that should he die Brutus would be his second choice. There was curiously nothing in his will concerning his son Caesarion.

Augustus, Rome's finest emperor.

After avenging Pompey, Caesar returned to Rome where he received four Triumphs, for his exploits in Gaul, Egypt, Asia and Africa. Triumphs were fabulous affairs, granted by the Senate. The person so honored rode through Rome on a chariot pulled by four horses, wearing a crown of laurels [something Caesar adored doing, as it covered his baldness] and a purple toga, his face painted red because he represented Jupiter as seen from old terracotta statues. Prisoners captured during the wars, as well as the victory spoils--armor, gold, silver, even paintings--led the march through the city. The most famous prisoner now was the Gaul Vercingetorix whom Caesar ordered publically throttled to death. He was just one of what Pliny said made up the 1,200,000 enemies Caesar had killed during the aforementioned campaigns. Even Cleopatra's sister Arsinoë was a captive, but thanks to the crowd's pleading, she was not put to death [although later her sister Cleopatra, fearful of her ambition, ordered Mark Antony to have her murdered]. Following the spoils came the senators and other nobles on foot, while his officers rode horseback nearby. Then came his soldiers, singing ribald songs, especially those concerning Caesar's sexual prowess, including his adventures with Nicomedes. They had the right to do so, and used it to the hilt, even though Caesar was visibly pained by the insults which inferred, of course, that he had been penetrated. He didn't seem to mind, however, the soldiers' warning to Romans to lock up their wives and daughters as protection against the bald fucker. In addition to the soldiers' songs there were clouds of incense and girls who dispersed flowers.

Caesar with Vercingetorix by
Lionel Royer.

As the cast was composed of thousands, prisoners included, there were incredible logistic problems, the least of which was housing and feeding of the masses. At night feasts were provided for the populace, 22,000 tables laden with the best food and wines. Then came the entertainment, days of more feasts, games, sporting events, gladiatorial fights, chariot races, as well as the killing of giraffes, seen for the first time in Rome, and 400 lions. Caesar worked during the gladiatorial fights, reading and signing petitions and laws that an endless stream of functionaries brought him, to the displeasure of the people, something that Octavian, who was there and observed the reaction of the spectators, would be careful to never do when he became emperor. But in Caesar's case it was proof that he simply never stopped working for his country [as Octavian, the future Augustus would also work unceasingly for Rome, later on]. A naval battle took place thanks to a lake dug next to the Tiber. The soldiers, despite their filthy ditties, received 5,000 denarii, more than they would have earned, Adrian Goldsworthy tells us in his superb book *Caesar*, in 16 years of service! Their leaders, the centurions, got 10,000 each. Notables were tipped 20,000 and each Roman 100 denarii, plus wheat and olive oil.

It was during the Lupercalia Festival that Mark Antony begged Caesar to become king. The festival was of pagan origin, held on the 15th of February, its purpose to purify the city from evil spirits. Interestingly, it was later called the Februatus, from the instruments used in the purification, the *febrva*, from which we've taken our February. Of Greek provenance, the festival was based on backwoods Arcadia and dedicated to Pan (1) and Pan's wolves, lupus, which pleased the Romans because it was a reminder of the she-wolf that had nursed Romulus and Remus. It was performed by boys, naked except for a goatskin enveloping the loins, boys who ran through the streets of Rome, slapping the hands that women held out, either in the hope that it would help them become pregnant or, if pregnant, that the pregnancy would pass well. The eroticism of the nude boys and the presence of girls who turned out numerous in order that their wishes be granted, inspired multiple couplings throughout the afternoon and night of the festival, and the certainty of an increase in the number of new Romans nine months later. It was during the festival that Mark Antony, dressed in nothing but the goatskin, approached Caesar, sitting on his gilded chair of office, and offered him, in front of a huge crowd, a crown, begging him to become king. Caesar refused and the crowd cheered. Antony offered the crown a second time and again it was refused, to even louder cheers. Some say that

Caesar was secretly disappointed, and that had the crowd showed enthusiasm for his kingship, he would have accepted it. Caesar's enemies tried to turn the moment against him by putting diadems on the heads of his statues, a sign of kingship aimed at alienating those who backed him. Antony and other followers immediately removed them, purportedly to Caesar's annoyance, as he'd found them to his liking.

He did not become a king but he would become a god at his death, a phenomenon that would become so automatic that when Vespasian was on his own deathbed, he joked, ''Oh, I think I'm becoming a god!''

The reasons for the conspiracy to murder him were as varied as the participants. Some thought that he had not accorded them sufficient honors, others hated his dictatorship, and although Sulla had been far more destructive, he had at least given up his dictatorship and returned home. Brutus seems to have been sincerely motivated by philosophical reasons, based on the reestablishment of the Republic. Cassius was thought to have been bitter because Brutus received so many honors from Caesar, and this due only to the fact that the boy was the son of Caesar's former mistress. Wall graffiti accused Brutus of doing nothing against the dictatorship, he who spoke so often about the joys of freedom. Goldsworthy states that once Brutus had decided to join the conspiracy his mind was made up, as it was in his character to be unshakeable. Even Caesar had said about him, ''Whatever Brutus wants, he wants badly.''

The Ides of March, the 15th, came and we have the Shakespearean warning as he made his way to the Senate, ''Beware of the Ides of March Caesar!'' ''The Ides of March have come,'' was Caesar's answer. ''Yes,'' said the soothsayer, ''but have not gone!'' The night before, Caesar had dined with his purported son, Brutus, and the topic of the best possible death was raised. Caesar had replied, ''For me, a sudden, unexpected death!''

His end was certainly unexpected and given other lingering forms of dying, one can say that it was sudden too. This man, who had worked as constantly as the ever-moving ocean for his country, was surrounded by the men he had raised to prominence, one perhaps his own boy or, at the very least, a boy he loved as his own, struck with hidden daggers, twenty-three thrusts and but four words, ''You too my son...''

The Death of Caesar by
Karl Theodor von Pilotz

It's amazing the sympathy many of us feel for fallen Caesar, who had nonetheless set Rome on the course of absolutism in the form of the future Roman Empire, while we deeply sympathize with Shakespeare's Mark Antony who turned all of Rome against the vile murderers of their assassinated dictator, murderers who nonetheless wished to preserve the Republic, assassins of one man who had killed at least two million others. We forget, too, that after the assassination the Senate, headed by Cicero, did all both could to bolster the powers of the assassins, especially those of Brutus and Cassius, providing them with arms, men and money to defeat Antony who had taken refuge in the East.

The Senate, encouraged by Cicero, sent out two armies under two Consuls to meet and defeat Antony's troops. They accomplished their mission and Rome and the Roman Republic appeared to have been saved, assuredly the case until ''fate intervened at the moment of victory,'' wrote historian Anthony Everett, ''and destroyed the best-laid plans.'' Both of the Consul-generals had been wounded during clashes with Antony's troops, and both eventually deceased, leaving Rome without Consuls and deprived of two victorious generals. Brutus was on the field too, but he was more a philosopher and bookworm than general, and sent word to the Senate that he lacked men, arms, cavalry, mules and money. At the same time, Antony received the help of Lucius Lepidus, whose troops Antony welcomed into his camp. [Lepidus was a statesman and general who ended up dying of despair when he learned that his wife was being bedded by Brutus' father during Lepidus' absence from Rome.] In the meantime, Cicero was in a self-delusional cocooned cuckooland. He declared victory before the Senate, praised Cassius in Asia Minor, and ordained a Triumph for Brutus. Octavian was still a teenager whom one and all dismissed in their calculations, especially as the boy showed every sign of conforming to the Senate's wishes, and had begun an exchange of letters with Cicero, both kissing the ass of the other, both claiming it smelled like roses. So the boy was ignored and the Senate, always ready to save money when it concerned the poor, reduced the pay of its soldiers, so certain were the senators of their victory. Cicero eventually woke up to the danger of underrating Octavian, and requested that the Senate vote him an ovation, just slightly less prestigious than a Triumph, a motion the Senate nonetheless voted down as unearned. Cicero's initiative even brought criticism from Brutus who found him too eager to please "the young friend of Caesar." [There had always been rumors that Octavian had been more than just Caesar's "young friend", notably because the boy was physically perfect, his face gorgeous. Cicero too had always been extremely partial to young handsome men, and although there were certain rumors concerning him and various lads, there was nothing at all of a concrete nature.] Cicero continued to be flattered that the heir to Caesar's fortune, now Caesar's adopted son, wrote intimately to him, requesting his advice and even inviting Cicero to share a Consulship with him. This set off alarm bells throughout the Senate because as Consul Octavian would have near-supreme powers, among them proscription. Proscriptions are difficult for the modern man to wrap his mind around, so I would like to pause a moment to discuss the phenomenon. They began with Sulla but became rampant devices of murder and pillage during the Second Triumvirate [the First Triumvirate had been organized by Pompey the Great, Caesar and Crassus for the purpose of uniting their forces in order to win elections and influence people]. The Second Triumvirate was between Marc Antony, Augustus [then called Octavian] and Lucius Lepidus. The purpose was to raise money to support the 43 legions necessary to hunt down and destroy Caesar's murderers, Brutus and Cassius. As stated earlier, because Antony and Augustus didn't trust each other, they met on an island, the riverbanks of which had 5,000 of Antony's soldiers on one side, 5,000 of Augustus' on the other. For two days, from dawn to dusk, they decided whom they would kill, either to loot their wealth or because they simply didn't like them. Lepidus sacrificed a brother, Augustus liquidated a former guardian. No relative or friend was spared, and many senators paid with their lives. Informers who denounced a man--any man could be denounced by wives and children in need of lucre, by creditors, former slaves, and neighbors who wanted a man's land- -were rewarded. Those who did the actual killing were given a part of the spoils. Even boys whose only guilt was having inherited money could find themselves on the list; they were immediately abandoned by their families and tracked like animals. Some men sought shelter down wells, in sewers, under rafters. The heads of victims were expedited to Antony who inspected them, at times, said one historian, over dinner. Augustus collected furniture, *objets d'art*, wonderful vases and priceless jewelry in this way. The Republic had truly come to an end, and a glorious exercise in democracy was buried for hundreds of years to come.

Octavian

Thunder struck when the boy led eight legions up to the walls of Rome. He sent a delegation with three demands, that he be named Consul, that his troops receive their full pay plus a bounty, and that all decrees against Mark Antony be repealed.

When the Senate hesitated, Octavian entered the city. He was given his Consulship [the youngest in Roman history, as he was still only 19], his army's bonus was doubled, senators tripped over themseles to do him honor, and Cicero belatedly agreed to a joint Consulship that the ''heaven-sent boy'', as Cicero called him, now laughed away. Octavian declared that the assassins of his ''father'' had committed a heinous crime, and a committee was set up to see that those responsilbe for it paid (4).

PART VI

ROME
ROMAN SEXUALITY

The marble glory that was Rome, characterized by its columned Forum, colosseum and baths that covered acres, were absent during the Republic, where chamber pots were emptied from windows and the wastes were carried away in channels in the middle of the streets. The first sewers had made their appearance, with water running under latrines were men sat side by side while discussing personal or political concerns, from 10 to 20 at a sitting, slaves posted to wipe their asses clean with sponges on the end of sticks. For every individual dwelling there were 26 apartment buildings, 3 to 5 stories high, that fell during torrential rains or earth quakes, and were ideal for the rapid spread of fires and disease.

The Forum was mile ''0'' to all the roads leading away from Rome, the nation's symbolic heart. Here the center of commerce, shops and fruit and vegetable stands, where men ''talked business and struck deals, discussed politics, reviewed legal cases with lawyers, listened to candidates' speeches, worshipped the gods and sacrificed to them, and cheered the victorious returning legions," wrote Francis Galassi in *Cataline*, 2014.

It was there that Sulla posted his list of proscriptions, men sentenced to murder, a price on their heads when brought in-- heads separated from their bodies. It was the highpoint of terror in Roman history, the fear of Sulla so great that he could walk through the streets unaccompanied by guards, his name evoked to frighten children into good behavior, a name men whispered when speaking to intimate friends, and this even long after his death through horrible suffering, his body infested by worms.

Sulla.
"No friend ever served me and no enemy ever wronged me, whom I have not repaid in full."
Sulla was pronounced dictator under a special law, the Lex Valeria, found in Appendix C.

The distribution of subventioned grain, that kept the urban poor from starvation and revolt, assured the elections of those who favored it, especially those who promised it would be free. The grain served to make bread and porridge, the staples of the people's diet. Fish was a luxury, pig the usual source of meat. Olives, olive oil and wine were plentiful, fruit and vegetables available, the most exotic for the tables of patricians.

The city and baths were furnished from aqueducts, the baths, a daily ritual, becoming bigger and more imposing during the reigns of the emperors. Only later, during the Middle Ages, were baths considered vectors of disease, the warm water opening the pores through which plague entered the body. The baths were frequented by women in the morning, men during the afternoon, a source of corporal and visual pleasure, where well-equipped gentlemen were openly applauded as they strode naked through the corridors, the key that opened the doors to luxurious and very private dinners.

Swamps surrounded the Eternal City, carriers of malaria, an extremely common disease, as were tuberculosis and typhoid fever. Summer was the season of death where, stated Pope Alexander VI, fat men died, the reason the rich abandoned the city for the high ground on nearby hills, where villas of wondrous beauty were built, from the time of the Republic to that of the emperors, especially Hadrian's Tibur complex (5).

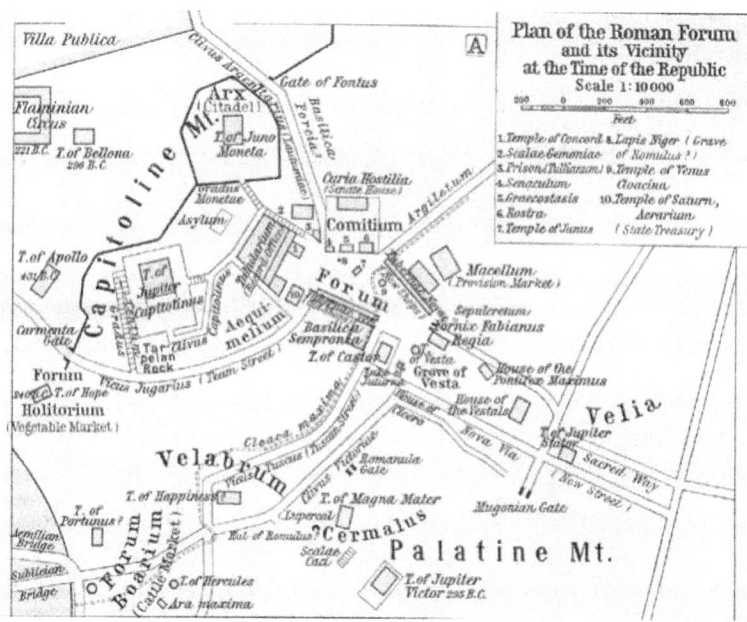

For centuries the Forum was the center of Roman life, where men met to converse and to conduct business and commercial affaires. They relieved themselves side by side while discussing the latest criminal trial, or perhaps wager on gladiatorial contests, more prized than our football today. They listened to speeches and could admire, breathless, majestic military Triumphs, followed by the obligatory public banquet, thousands of tables laden with food and drink. Even during pre-Colosseum times marble columned buildings and temples were awe-inspiring, as were statues like those to Castor and Pollux, admired by provincials who came to see the world's most beautiful city, whose ruins, even in our times, are visited by 5 million sightseers yearly.

Habitations surrounding the Forum were all equipped with balconies so those wealthy enough could watch the daily crowds, a spectacle in itself, as well as the games later moved to the Colosseum.

The Forum was the scene of revolts, slaughter and the lynching of Tiberius Gracchus while his followers were clubbed to death.

All young nobles were expected to offer their maiden speeches at the Forum Rostra, and it was there that Cicero warned the people against Catiline's followers, and where Marc Antony eulogized Caesar.

Unlike today, men lived longer than women, perhaps to age 40 or 50, if not killed during wars, which was a common source of early death, by battle wounds or by horrifying dysentery. Mortality among children remained high until age 10. Romans practiced burials and cremations, the poor dumped in open pits, the rich in decorated tombs. A living could be made as a professional mourner, accompanying a patrician's body to its final resting place, while dead slaves were discarded like rubbish, to be hauled away to graves. Slaves were provided for by their masters, especially freed slaves, and the poor were cremated and placed in a columbarium, niches in subterranean structures, their names and perhaps an epigraph on stone placed over the site. Columbariums were visited and flowers offered.

A Via Appia Columbarium

ROMAN SEXUALITY

Senators were regularly excluded from the Senate due to ''gross immorality'', which basically meant the financial plundering of offices, usually in the provinces and further abroad, although such plundering was part of the rewards given to Consuls and magistrates who had served unpaid in Rome. So the abuse had to be flagrant, often accompanied by accusations of murder, for the Senate to go to the extreme measure of banishing one of its own.

Sexual abuse was also a possibility covered by the term ''gross immorality'', although here too every man, or nearly every man, was using his position for sexual gain, a proclivity that gained notoriety under certain emperors, and has continued to this very day with Roman cardinals and popes, the most notorious of which was Pope Alexander VI (7).

For this reason we will now have a look into Roman sexuality, that I'll compare with what took place in Greece, as Romans were noted for copying everything Greek.

All historical sources conclude that the Romans couldn't care less if a man stuck his dick in a girl or a boy: it just didn't matter. Caesar himself was known to be a man to every woman, a woman to every man. His soldiers sang ditties to that effect as they marched along, perhaps not always to Caesar's amusement; in fact, Caesar was far more sensitive about losing his hair than how he'd lost his cherry, when young, to King Nicomedes who happened to have been a Bithynian like Antinous, and like

Antinous Nicomedes was noted for the dimensions of his member. The words hetero and homo didn't exist yet because the distinction between them was immaterial.

Priapus and His Weight in Gold mural scene

Whereas Greek boys were encouraged to have older lovers and to learn from them, the Romans had sex for pleasure as long as the participants respected two iron-clad principles (although, as we all well know, all iron-clad principles are made to be disregarded): A Roman male could not have sex with another Roman male. If he was horny and a slave (or a foreigner or anyone else, as long as he wasn't a Roman) passed by, he was fair game. The second principle was that a Roman male had to do the penetrating. It was he who was *vir*ile (*vir* meaning manly in Latin). A corollary to the two principles was the very strong preference for young smooth hairless bodies, often between the ages of 14 and 20, marked by the onset of down on the boy's cheeks (permissible too on his butt cheeks). Greek boys had Greek lovers, often many, from whom the boys gained the key to life: *knowledge*. The boys were normally passive, the men active, and when the boys became men, the roles were inversed: they took on a boy of their own, their belovèd, and they became the boy's lover and teacher. There was also a practical side to Greek love. A lover would never ever show weakness before his belovèd and vice versa, which made them the fiercest fighting force the world has ever known.

The Romans and Greeks practiced intercrural insertion and vaginal and anal penetration, but fellatio and cunnilingus were rare. Mutual masturbation and circle jerks were hardly ever mentioned because they were so common between schoolboys, a little like boys pissing together, and perhaps also because this took place between Roman boys. Greek parents despaired of keeping their sons, if they were beautiful, chaste. Roman boys had access to slaves, as their elders did, on whom they could practice intercourse, intercrural or anal. As today, the Romans associated male/male relations with Greece (in France one says, for the English Go Fuck Yourself: *Va te faire voir chez les Grecs*). In the same way that one drinks anything when thirsty or eats the food offered when hungry, one will go with any male slave or foreigner when he has a hard-on. Diogenes the Cynic says that of the three appetites, food, drink and sex, sex is the easiest to fulfill as one need only rub oneself to obtain instant satisfaction.

Sex was found in brothels and latrines and taverns, parks and gardens and any other place sheltered from public view. Hadrian's successor, Lucius Verus, opened a tavern in his own home in order to create a climate for debauch. Male prostitutes showed their wares in parks and gardens as they do today, and many turned to acting to supplement their incomes, as did Hadrian's favorite Pylades.

Lucius Verus

As just being a wife was enough status for most women, men were free to look elsewhere for pleasure. In Rome love was always in the air. The Romans had adopted many of the Greek gods and their myths, especially those which dealt with Apollo and Hyacinth, Hercules and Hylas, Achilles and Patroclus, Zeus and his cupbearer and bedmate Ganymede. Antinous' role was strikingly similar to that played by Ganymede, and as he was Greek he was a safe foreigner, although it's doubtful that Hadrian would have turned him away should he have been a Roman citizen. The Greeks were not obliged to look for sex in gardens or taverns or back alleys. They had gymnasiums where they could openly entice boys, although not those under age 18. Rich parents sent slaves to accompany their sons to and from the gym. Sex between boys was so current that we have the story of the Greek boy who didn't share his schoolmates' interest in men. He prayed to Zeus so that he too could be moved by the love of boys, but when this failed to happen, he committed suicide.

Two men, one woman--mural

A huge difference between the Greeks and the Romans [if historians, after two thousand years, are correct; let us not forget that there isn't one word in Homer concerning homosexual relationships] was that the Greeks preferred their boys with modest members, the perfect size to fit the anus and the mouth, whereas the Romans followed the cult of Priapus, and, as today, thought that bigger was always better. Supposedly, clapping could be heard in the Roman baths when a man of healthy dimensions paraded through the corridors, as mentioned earlier. One Roman, Cotta, was known to invite only guests to his lavish dinners whom he had first seen at the baths--a word often on his lips was donkey. Presumably, even heteros today show deferential admiration for those who show more manliness than they do themselves, which does not necessarily have anything to do with the desire to be penetrated. Roman boys often wore phallic amulets to protect them from the evil eye, and even today Roman men and boys quickly touch their balls to ward off evil, as when, for example, they see a passing priest.

Some hoopla developed concerning the roles of the Greek lover and his beloved. Lovers didn't just fall in love with any boy, but only those who showed intelligence and maturity. The sexual link was ephemeral and came to an end with the growing of a first beard. From then on the boy and lover became loyal friends and remained so throughout their lives. Love was to be simple and undebauched, built on education and physical maintenance. But if this were true, wondered Cicero, why did lovers only fall in love with handsome youths and never ugly ones?

Boys, then as now, were mantraps: The poet Tibullus tells us that we have no chance against tender youths, who give us ample reason to love them. This boy is pleasing due to the masterly control he has over his horse; this other one causes our hearts to flutter when he breaks the surface of the water, showing his snow-white chest and nipples; so and so captures us by his daring; such and such by his peaches-and-cream complexion. At times youths objected for the form when men made advances, even menacing to tell their fathers if the men didn't cease. But once bridled, and the man could find rest after expulsing his lust, it was the boy who sought more, awaking the man from sleep by the gentle entreating of his buttocks. Again satisfied, man and boy plunged back into the arms of Morpheus for an hour before the boy asked if the man would like to do it again. The man did, but when the boy stirred still again, an hour later, it was the man who threatened the boy, ''If you don't stop I'll tell your daddy!''

Pan and Nymph

Boys also lacked fidelity, as in this letter sent from one Kurnos, a Greek, to his lover Timaleus, away at war. ''Dear Timaleus, it is I, Kurnos. Many a friend has come and gone since you left, but it is to you that my thoughts return. Whenever I see Themis' horses, I think of my friend Timaleus. Remember how we stole rides before Eos' early light, and galloped across the fields like a single rider on his dapple mare--I've quite forgotten her name. She's grown too old to support one as sturdy as I, but she foaled just after you went away, and the little colt has long since borne my weight. Do you regret my sending you on campaign? I only stayed a month with Saurus and from then after missed only you. Come back home, my dear friend, and do not upbraid me harshly, for it is as the poet said: 'Boys and horses are the same. A horse does not cry for his rider thrown into the dust, but carries another man and eats his corn; a boy, too, only loves his current friend.' ''

The role of a boy wasn't always easy either. Men liked them soft enough to caress, but not so soft as to be effeminate. Boys might relish being penetrated, but not enough to be mistaken for a woman. If the boy seemed too eager he could open himself to abuse, as men abused girls who were too available. Boys were often believed to be easily impaled because the anal muscles were supple, due to the fact that they hadn't as yet turned into real men. But rent-boys were often called upon to sodomize men who lusted for anal contact, as they had when young, because their anuses itched for what only a penis could scratch.

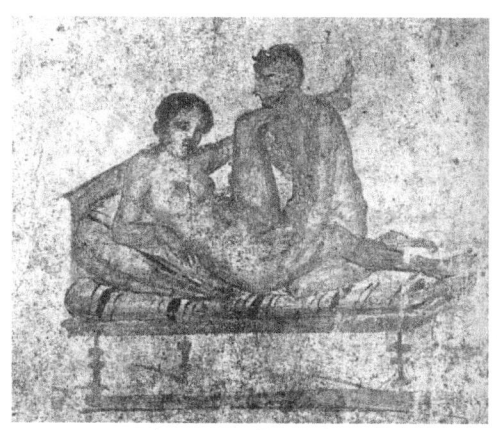

A mural scene

Fellatio and cunnilingus were both looked down upon as being unclean [as if sodomy were any better]. The former, fellatio, was often associated with grown men with beards. Women were there for fucking, boys for sodomy and bearded men for cock sucking. Another degrading aspect was the use of sex to further one's advancement. From multiple sources we learn that this was Hadrian's way with Trajan's entourage: he advanced through screwing the emperor's influential friends, and by being screwed by them. But given the known promiscuous nature of Trajan's court, and the incredible sexual arousal in a climate of lustful males, most of whom were not simply Trajan's buddies but youths recruited to fulfill the needs of the emperor and his associates, Hadrian's task had certainly not been arduous.

Socrates warns about kissing Alcibiades' handsome son: "The beast they call young and handsome is more dangerous than a scorpion. You needn't touch a boy as you do a scorpion to be poisoned. A boy, with just a look, can make you mad from a distance. So when you see a beautiful boy run for your life, take a year's holiday elsewhere as it will take that long to heal you."

The Greek ideal of how fathers should raise their sons was, as usual, based on the gods. Zeus, for example, had excellent relations with his sons Hermes and Apollo. Here a poet reveals a scene in which Zeus is explaining to Apollo just how smart Hermes is: " 'I've never seen anyone so clever. A while back, for instance, Hermes and I were scrounging around Earth on some business or other--no, not what you're thinking; there were no petticoats involved--and being hungry and tired we stopped in at a peasant's hut along the way. Well, Son, you know how lowly and miserably those humans live. I had to destroy them once by sending that great flood, so sick had I become of seeing their despicable ways. I can't figure it out. They have everything to make them happy: physically they are as perfectly formed and as sound as are we; they have the same brain and heart; it should be as easy for them to love and be loved as it is for us. But what do we see on Earth? Tortured faces, worried expressions, selfish acts. I could forgive them their weaknesses were they to at least take part in life. But no. They scurry around like sheep, their heads down for fear the heavens may fall. And when Death beckons, they trudge off to the cold blackness of the tomb, they who could have known light, warmth and laughter during their ephemeral existence

''Anyway,'' continued Zeus, ''Hermes and I stopped at some peasant's hovel and to our astonishment we were hospitably offered warm wine and vittles. To thank the old man, Hermes and I asked him to confide his heart's innermost wish. The poor old fellow sighed and said that although he was impotent and his wife long dead, his heart's desire was to have a son.

''Now, I would have instructed him to eat a certain potent mushroom that has wondrous regenerative powers and then get himself a mistress. But not Hermes. After some thought he told the old man to go to his wife's grave and take out her bones. He was then to sacrifice a bull to Almighty Myself, skin the hide into which he would place his wife's bones, piss on the remains, and bury the hide and its contents in his wife's grave. At the end of nine months he was to return and dig it all up.

''The old man did as instructed, and when he returned nine months later he found a boy at the bottom of the pit, swaddled in the old hide. We named him 'Orion', which is Greek for 'He-Who-Makes-Water' and, by extension, urine.' '' (1)

In the ancient world, as today, boys and men knew pining, tears, longing, despair, self-sacrifice--the entire panoply of sentiments. In Thebes the Sacred Band was formed, 300 lovers and their belovèds, fed at public expense and housed on the acropolis, they formed a group of warriors who would sacrifice themselves at the snap of a finger for their companions. Love between men was so special in Thebes that it was, says Plato, illegal for anyone to maintain that sex between men was not beautiful. Thanks to the Sacred Band Thebes freed itself from Spartan domination, until it was totally destroyed by Alexander the Great, he who was said to have known defeat only once in his life, when confronting the thighs of his lover Hephaestion.

Naturally, had there been only homosexuals in Thebes, Thebans would have died out. Plutarch relates the story of a rich Theban woman who arranged the kidnapping of a handsome ephebe that she then kept at her side until he understood that she was as interested in his welfare as she was her sexual satisfaction. She married the lad, to the fury of his male suitors. [This brings to mind the wonderful scene in *Some Like It Hot* in which Jack Lemmon returns from his date with Osgood and declares to Tony Curtis that they're going to get married. ''But why would a guy marry another guy?'' asked Curtis. ''For *security!''* exclaims Lemmon.] There is also the story of Heracles' passage through Thebes where he slept, during a single night, with the forty-nine virgin daughters of the same father. The fiftieth daughter refused him and in anger he sentenced her to remain a virgin until the end of her life. Girls, however, got the best of Heracles when his boyfriend, the beautiful Hylas, abandoned him for nymphs that resided in a spring [which may have meant, in reality, that at some time during their relationship Hylas accidently drowned].

At any rate, a good father always had a ready tale for his son's ears. Zeus told Hermes about the Trojan War, but as the story was long and the boy appeared to be asleep ... well ... let the poet finish: ''Almighty Zeus interrupted his story and looked down at this son. Hermes' arm and head rested unmoving on Zeus' leg. Zeus thought he had fallen asleep, and softly tried to disengage himself. But Hermes raised his head. There was the same look of intelligence and anticipation, although with anxiety least Almighty Father wish not to continue. Zeus hadn't the heart to abridge his promise to tell the story of the Great War. So after taking a few moments out while he put more tree trunks on the fire, stopped the moon and stars in their course and issued orders to Sleep--who owed him a favor--to make this night thrice, he returned to his throne, Hermes again at this knees, and while running his fingers through his son's auburn locks, Almighty Father picked up the thread of his tale without the loss of a single strand.'' (1)

Augustus continually tongue-whipped the nobility because they weren't showing the example to the people by producing more progeny, which meant more farmers, more government servants and, especially, more soldiers. It must never be forgotten that for Rome incessant war was a source of wealth in various goods, land [especially land for soldiers upon their retirement], agricultural products and slaves--slaves that ran the economy thanks to their work, but also because they were often the teachers and philosophers who gave direction to Roman life and culture.

Hadrian was absorbed by mysticism, the occult, fortune telling and conjurers who could not only caste the spells that could bring one a lover or assure the death of an enemy, but could also help in one's sexual performance--supernatural aphrodisiacs. Pornography was an aid and walls were often covered with erotic frescos. Prostitution was legal, public and practiced everywhere. Males were naturally attracted to boys as well as girls, and it must not be forgotten that words for homosexual or heterosexual didn't exist in any form, although there were words for effeminacy. Again: virility comes from the Latin *vir* meaning manly, but is also found in the word virtue, meaning that it was appropriate to control one's sexual appetites.

Pederasty referred to, in ancient Greece, young men, not young boys. There was, naturally, no *legal* age in Greece. The boys involved were military age, which infers that they had left boyhood. In Greece pederasty was simply the socially accepted erotic friendship between a man and a boy, a boy being between the ages of 15 to 17 [many Greek poets refer to 16 as the perfect age for the belovèd]. In Crete it seems to have been a vital ingredient in military life, sanctioned by Zeus himself, an active pederast. Still, many scholars have found it strange that it was not commented on at all in Homer [a reason, perhaps, why Hadrian eventually turned away from Homer to the benefit of other writers such as Herodotus, Plato, Athenaeus and Xenophon-- whom Hadrian adored (5)]. In all other aspects of Greek life pederasty was clearly apparent: nude athletics, nude sculptures of ephebes [kouroi], historically famous cohorts of men and boys such as the Sacred Band of Thebes, as well as--with very few exceptions--the utter exclusion of women.

From this distance in time it's hard to pin down the behavior of the. Some poets claim that his role was passive in the sense that he contented himself with being beautiful, looking meekly at the ground as his lover greats him, allowing the man to stroke his cheek and gently nudge his genitals through the boy's chiton, the light tunic he wore that fell to the knees. Today this would seem erotic and daring, but also how arousing! Perhaps the lad did feel he had to play a submissive role, but I'm sure all masks fell away while he was being, later and in private, tenderly caressed by his lover.

Greek chiton

In Crete a boy seems to have been abducted by a lover who, in concord with the boy's friends, takes the lad into the countryside where they spend two idyllic months hunting, feasting and exhausting their young bodies. The belovèd is then returned home with the symbolic gifts of military dress, an ox and a drinking cup [and whatever else the man might wish him to have, gifts the expense of which would depend on the man's resources]. Interestingly, the boy was then known by a Greek word meaning ''he who stands ready,'' perhaps signifying Ganymede who, after being abducted by Zeus, stood ready, at the god's side, to serve him food and drink. It's interesting too to note that the boy's father was keep informed of each stage of his son's abduction and, indeed, his great wish was to have a son who would be handsome enough to attract a suitable suitor--one influential enough to give the boy a boost into the better classes, knowing full well that his boy would be the object of sexual passion, as the father had himself been as a boy.

Boys in Greece were free to choose their suitors, while the boys' sisters had to comply with their father's wishes, wishes based on political and economic advantages. The boys received continual gifts and tender attention from their lovers, the girls were paid for and sent to the kitchen or the bed according to their husband's needs. Girls remained virgin until marriage and remained loyal to their husbands. Boys could have as many relationships with other boys and men as they wished, each serving as a step upwards in the boys' advancement through society. As related, the same was true for Hadrian who sought influence with Trajan by plowing the buttocks of the emperor's consorts or allowing access to his own. In Athens as well as in Rome boys and their multiple lovers remained friends, often throughout their entire lives.

Prostitutes served as an alternate form of sexual outlet. Romans and Greeks had the choice of women, girls, wives, men, boys and pleasuring themselves. The only difference, as said, was that Roman men could not have sex with other Roman men or women [other than one's own wife or husband], but only with foreigners, slaves and prostitutes--a rule certainly broken on occasion. And they had to be the top, in today's parlance, never the bottom. In Greece anything went down as normal and good, although throughout all time the penetrator has always been more respected than the penetrated. Prostitutes were looked down upon and Roman or Greek nobles thought to have sold their wares were tainted through the rest of their lives. Caesar himself never lived down the accusation, certainly true, that he was King Nicomedes' boy while ambassador to Bithynia. In Athens the politician Aeschines lost power when accused of having been a rent-boy in his youth.

Virtus, manliness, was the quality that drove the Roman state and gave the Romans *imperium*, power, over their women, over foreigners and foreign countries, and over their slaves. This manliness was tied to sexual dominance. A Roman man was expected to penetrate the rest of the world as he did a mistress and his boys, and it was he who would decide who would be allowed to penetrate the females in his household.

As in relationships today, then, too, one could turn on one's lover. There is the example of Philip of Macedon, Alexander the Great's father. When Philip was a boy he was sent to Thebes and placed under the care of Pammenes, a great general and boy-lover who immediately reserved the young and willing prince for his bed. Pammenes is known for criticizing Nestor's role in the Trojan War because Nestor organized the men according to their country and not in groups of lovers and their belovèds, groups that would have fought to the death before letting down their loved-ones. No act was more valued than giving one's life for one's belovèd.

Later, when Philip was king of Macedon, his general Pausanias came to him with the complaint that he had been forcefully sodomized. Pausanias felt that he had the king's ear because they had been lovers when young. Pausanias claimed that he had had relations with a boy who killed himself when Pausanias threw him over for another. The boy's former lover, a certain Attalus, decided to wreck vengeance on Pausanias by inviting him to a banquet, during which he forcefully raped Pausanias after getting him drunk. Pausanias hoped that King Philip would avenge the outrage by killing Attalus, but Attalus was both an essential general in Philip's army and the father of Philip's wife. So to placate Pausanias, Philip named him to his personal guard, affording Pausanias the proximity he needed to drive a dagger into Philip's chest--thus opening the way for

Philip's son, the Great Alexander. Pausanias, in turn, was cut down by the rest of Philip's guard.

In Plato's *Symposium* we learn that man-and-boy love was advantageous because no army could overcome the bond between lovers, and it worked in the favor of democracy because no despotic ruler was more powerful than the loyalty between men and their boys. We have the case of Harmodius and Aristogeiton: Hippias and Hipparchus were joint dictators in Athens. Hipparchus fancied Harmodius who refused his advances. To gain revenge, Hipparchus refused to let Harmodius' sister take part in the Panathenaea Games, accusing her of not being a virgin, a requirement for the games. Harmodius and his lover Aristogeiton decided to rid Athens of the dictatorship and thusly redeem the honor of Harmodius' sister. With daggers hidden in their chitons, the boys fell on Hipparchus at the foot of the Acropolis, stabbing him to death. Hipparchus' guards immediately killed Harmodius and Aristogeiton was captured. While being tortured to reveal any coconspirators, Aristogeiton promised to tell the truth if Hippias would give him clemency, sealed with a handshake. When Hippias complied, Aristogeiton laughed at his having shaken the hand of his own brother's murderer. Hippias, mad with fury, thrust his dagger into Aristogeiton's throat (3).

Plato claimed that the ideal nation would be based on lovers, because no lover would ever dishonor his beloved. To the contrary, he would do everything in his power to build him up, to educate him, to do for him all that was virtuous and good and honorable. All the great gods, all of them with the one exception of Ares, god of war, were lovers to their belovèds. [Ares was too unfeeling to appreciate tender friendships: he killed and maimed, maddening men so they would take nursing babies from their mothers and dash their brains against walls or tree trunks.] The poet Theognis justified his own love of boys by relating, to friends, the story of how Zeus had abducted Ganymede. As in Rome, the Greeks too were unaware of the concept of sexual orientation. Men quite simply did what they wanted to do. Only the role in the act was of importance. In Rome and in Athens the penetrator was masculine, adult and of high social status; the penetrated was a youth or, if not, he was categorized as being effeminate or socially inferior. Not only did men share a sexual relationship with boys, they saw to it that boys were educated in the Greek way, meaning in the responsibilities that would be theirs in manhood. The period between the moment the man took a liking to a boy and the moment he quenched his desire, could be several weeks or months, giving the youth time to assure himself that the man had a genuine attachment for him, one that surpassed sexual lust. Normally the youth had body hair, but cases of boys being appropriated at age 12 were not unknown.

Such was Patroclus' role with his beloved Achilles: friend, teacher and protector. The poet enters their sleeping chamber: ''Both arranged their clothes. Achilles slipped into the bed the first, and then Patroclus. Patroclus found his place against Achilles' side, his leg gently draped over his beloved's thighs. Did Patroclus foresee his coming fate, a fate he knew he held in common with others, as he held in common the happiness that filled his heart at this moment, a happiness that was his, but one that others had known and would know again, and that long after he had become dust? He put his arm under his beloved's head and leaned over him. Silently he searched the blue eyes, and finding his answer, he kissed the parted lips. Then he moved his head back and with one breath blew out the oil lamp, bringing down night, a celestial curtain.'' (1)

In Rome men may have preferred the passive role, desiring to be penetrated by their slaves, but such men were not considered as being *vir*, real-men: only the penetration of a handsome youth, by a man, was judged conventional. The use of perfume and cosmetics and others forms of effeminacy were tolerated by some men when they concerned youths, but not adult men. Roman boys and men were allowed male-slave-sexual-partners as a way of discharging their lust, an alternative form to pleasuring oneself. The male-slave-sexual-partner was generally replaced, sooner or later, by a wife. The slave would then cut his hair short and join the domain of the other slaves. A slave boy could be castrated to preserve a youthful aspect, as Nero had castrated Sporus before marrying him. Naturally, slaves could service their mistresses as well as their masters. As with Caesar [and King Nicomedes], Roman males often went through stages during which they evolved from being sexually passive to sexually active. In one well-known case, involving a youth who did not manage the transition from passive to active, his father, Quintus Fabius Maximus Eburnus, had his son killed for being "unchaste." The hypocrisy of the matter was that as a youth Fabius himself had been called a "chick", signifying a boy-love-object, known for his good looks and availability. His reaction towards his son was perhaps a counter-reaction against his own juvenile misdeeds. The satirist Juvenal states that male prostitutes were found in streets known to all, as well as the baths, especially valued as one could check out the potential of what one was buying. As previously mentioned, the key word for most same-sex-enthusiasts was "hung". Apuleius, the irreverent writer of *The Golden Ass*, mentions a banquet in the midst of which a *"well-endowed"* young man was fellated by all the participants.

Same-sex marriages were not legally recognized in Rome. The aforementioned Juvenal criticized them because he felt that one day they would be legalized. Nero purportedly married several men, Pythagoras and Sporus among them. Nero was the bride and wore a bridal veil, the men received a substantial dowry. Cicero accused Mark Antony of being a slut in his youth and married to one Curio. This is one among many reasons why Antony insisted on Cicero's death the moment Antony gained power. The exquisite Emperor Elagabalus is reported to have married his charioteer, Hierocles, and the athlete Zoticus. He was assassinated at age 18.

Rapists were subject to death if they raped a woman, boy or man. Slaves, prostitutes and entertainers were public property, and as such couldn't be raped [even up to Shakespeare's time actors often rounded off their monthly earnings through prostitution]. A man who was raped [anally or orally] was legally exempt from public stigma. It goes without saying that rape was the perfect vengeance, and according to some sources it occurred as often between men as it did between men and women among the Romans. When it happened to a Roman citizen it was thought to equal, in horror, parricide, the rape of a virgin or the robbing of a temple.

Augustus banned soldiers from marrying, a ban that held good for 200 years. Soldiers could not have sex among themselves in the same way that no Roman citizen could have sex with another Roman citizen outside of marriage. Many took mistresses and had children that they recognized after leaving the service. All turned to prostitutes of both sexes and gang rapes followed military conquests. As with all other Roman citizens, a man was forbidden to lose his masculinity by allowing his body to be violated. The historian Polybius wrote that a soldier found guilty of being penetrated was clubbed to death. Plutarch recounts the story of the handsome recruit who was pursued by his commanding officer. He shunned the unwanted advances until the officer ordered him to bend over. The recruit drew his sword and plunged it into the chest of the commander. Not only wasn't the recruit sentenced to death, the mandatory sentence, he was awarded the Crown for Bravery, the equivalent of today's Medal of Honor.

It seems evident that due to the multiple ways of appeasing one's lust, Roman males put off marriage. Naturally, if a woman was of the high nobility and wealthy, she didn't remain without a husband for long, but with husbands seeking release with young girls and boys who were foreigners, slaves and/or prostitutes, and with one entering into adultery as freely and guiltlessly as did the Romans, the birth rate diminished to such an extent that the great Augustus never stopped chewing out the men who frequented his court. Finally, laws were drawn up, forcing men to marry at the very latest between the ages of 25 and 30, and to produce a child before age 26 if they wished to escape penalties. Women were to marry between ages 20 and 30, giving birth during her twentieth year. Men who fathered three children or more received rewards and rapid career advancement. As boys sought fortune by giving themselves to older men [an example being Mark Antony and the wealthy Curio whose relationship lasted so long that it was considered an unofficial marriage by some] in hopes of a rapid and rich inheritance, a law was passed allowing such legacies only from close relatives. Widows were obliged to marry within two years of their husbands' deaths and divorcees within 18 months. Also, Augustus, knowing that theaters were the preferred sites for men who hoped to waylay boys, set aside special sections where the boys could be accompanied by chaperons, an extremely difficult task as handsome boys always found a way to please men who knew the art of flattery and knew of boys' ever-present need for the sound of sweet jangling pocket change. Of course, Augustus too had been a beautiful boy and had certainly had his share of suitors. Where before one had looked the other way concerning adultery, now adulterers were punished with banishment or flogging. Augustus had his daughter Julia sent to rot on an island, as she was found to have spread her thighs for literally any virile male. Male/male relations were never punished, but the loss of one's seed between a boy's buttocks or through autoeroticism were considered a waste in times when the state needed kids, and plenty of them.

While Augustus lived a life of moderation in food, surroundings and sex, Rome--like Florence during the Renaissance--was more and more enticed by Hellenistic pederasty, although Roman sex often included men-on-men sex to a far greater degree than did the Greeks whose ideal was always boys and youths. Patrons like Maecenas, and other wealthy boy-loving Hellenists, assured the survival of generations of poets, Martial, Catullus, Horace, Virgil and others, certainly because they loved art, but perhaps also in exchange for unrecorded sexual favors. We're told that Hadrian often drank and loved boys, but that he was never drunk and that he had never ever harmed a lad. The general, historian and poet Arrian, sent to Cappadocia by Hadrian, wrote the life of Alexander and gave advice in the Stoic tradition, advising against taking up with ballet boys but counseled that one should take one's pleasure decently with both sexes. Graffiti found from that time describes a cobbler and a rope maker who lived together and were buried together.

Lucius Apuleius is known for his book the *Golden Ass* in which a sorcerer accidently turns himself into an ass and has all kinds of Boccaccio-like adventures; but he's also noted for his youthful love poems that he read to boys in order to gain their favors. His own life was quite an adventure: He studied in Carthage, Athens and Rome where he was a lawyer. He then went off to Asia and Egypt to study philosophy and various cults, becoming even a priest of Isis. During his travels he met a very wealthy widow whose hand he won, through magic spells and charms, said her family when they found out they were no longer in her will. Later, he read his works in public and organized gladiatorial events, both of which won him great popularity. At the end of the *Golden Ass* the sorcerer changed back into a man by eating roses--the well-known antidote for those changed into asses--but was ill received by his lover who had preferred him as an ass with a huge member (8).

PART VII

CATILINE'S WICKED WAYS

Although Catiline had taken no part in the Civil War that brought Sulla to power, his brother-in-law, Marcus Marius Gratidianus had fought against Sulla, which meant that Sulla would put him on the list of men to be proscribed, something Sulla hadn't yet done. In order to escape being contaminated by his relationship with Gratidianus, Catiline decided to murder him, thusly gaining credit in Sulla's eyes. In this he was aided by Quintus Lutatius Catulus [called Capitolinus because he had the same name as his father, a strong supporter of Sulla in the Civil War]. Quintus wanted to avenge his father who, when Gratidianus threatened to prosecute him over his affiliation with Sulla [when Sulla was in exile], committed suicide. Both knew that Sulla would eventually kill Gratidianus and take his property, but they decided not to wait. They lured Gratidianus to a site where he was bound and pulled to the grave of Catulus-*père*, over which they broke his limbs "and gouged out his eyes", wrote Sallust, before beheading him. Catiline then carried the head through Roman streets to where Sulla was holding court, and presented it to him.

Catiline fell in love with a whore, Aurelia Orestilla, whom no respectable man would touch. She hesitated to marry him for fear that his son from an earlier marriage would oppose the union, which caused Catiline to murder the boy "in order to clear the house of an impediment", wrote Sallust. After the murder, continued Sallust, he found no rest, "so cruelly did remorse torture his frenzied soul. His complexion became pallid, his yes hideous." Cicero later accused him of the murders on the floor of the Senate, shouting into his face, "Not a long time has passed since you freed your house with the death of your first wife to welcome a second one. And did you not add a second crime, far worse than the first? I had better not insist, so that no one will know that in our city such a terrifying crime has been left unpunished."

In 73 B.C. Catiline was accused of bedding a Vestal Virgin, a woman who was sworn to chastity, a woman who represented Vesta, goddess of the hearth, home and family. She was considered to be the daughter of Rome, a person both powerful and venerated, of great historical, political and religious importance. The Virgin in question, recounts the historian Asconius, was Fabia, who just happened to have been the half-sister of Cicero's wife Terentia. In fucking a Vestal Virgin Catiline was fucking Rome, an intolerable desecration, for which the man was whipped to death, the woman immured with food, enough to keep her alive for as long as possible before dying of starvation.

He was defended by Catulus, his cohort in murder, and exonerated.

Although sexual congress with girls and boys was common, with boys it was less so than in Greek times, and indeed, it was forbidden under pain of death between men in the army, although perhaps tolerated to some degree because Caesar had sported with King Nicomedes and did so later with men and boys, which left him open to songs of vile content, and winks between commanders when a recruit was seen slipping into his field tent. Cicero's mocking of Catiline for his sexual abuse of highbred aristocratic lads even reached the Senate floor, when Cicero spoke of "Catiline's special bodyguard, friends he embraces and takes to his bosom, whom you see with carefully combed hair, beardless or with well-trimmed beards, clothed with veils, not with robes, whose labor is expended in suppers lasting till daybreak. These boys, so witty and delicate, have learned not only to love and to be loved, not only to sing and to dance, but also to brandish daggers and to administer poisons. What do these wretches want? Are they going to take their wives with them to the camp? How can they do without them, especially at night, and how will they endure the Apennines, and these fronts, and this snow, unless they think that they will bear the winter more easily because they have been in the habit of dancing naked at their feasts? War isn't to be dreaded, when Catiline surrounds himself with a bodyguard of prostitutes!''

His lust, declared Cicero, included gladiators and those ''on stage'', including ''indulging in infamous love of others, and encouraged their infamous affection for himself.''

The total of Sallust's commentary on Catiline covers 58 pages.
About Catiline Sallust states: ''Of noble birth, he had a powerful intellect and great physical strength, but a vicious and depraved nature. From his youth he had delighted in civil war, bloodshed, robbery and political strife. He could endure hunger, cold and want of sleep to an incredible extent. His mind was daring, crafty, capable of any pretense and dissimilation. A man of flaming passions, he was as covetous of other men's possessions as he was prodigal of his own. He was an eloquent speaker but lacked wisdom.''
Sallust goes on to say that Catiline surrounded himself with criminals, debauchees, murderers, gamblers, cut-throats, anyone who was morally bankrupt or financially bankrupt.

His preferred company was young men whom some, especially Cicero, stated he performed lewd acts, the younger the more easily the boys were impressionable and easily ensnared. He gratified them with mistresses, horses and dogs, and put them under his obligation by loans of money. He taught the youths how to forge documents and commit perjury convincingly, and in order to occupy them he had them commit outrages, even killings.

PART VIII

CATILINE'S CONSPIRACIES

Because what follows is based on Sallust's book *The Conspiracy of Catiline*, the moment has come to introduce this wonderful person.

Sallust [Gaius Sallustius Crispus] was born in 86 B.C. and died in 35 B.C., his last years spent in writing histories, the first of which was *The Conspiracy of Catiline*, our prime source, of immense importance because Sallust knew Catiline personally. A Tribune in 52 B.C., he automatically became a member of the Senate, from which he was expelled in 50 B.C., possibly due to some form of financial extortion [corruption was universal among senators then as it is today]. His lucky star was the rise of Caesar, whom he served in various military campaigns and who assured his re-entry into the Senate. Caesar awarded him the governorship of a province in North Africa [*Africa nova*, basically what had been ancient Carthage--the name of the province eventually applied to the entire continent]. Sallust was said to have disgracefully pillaged the province, but sources at the time claimed he was forgiven by Caesar in return for a consequent bribe. He had a villa at Tivoli and a mansion with park in Rome. He retired immediately after the death of his benefactor, Caesar, sign of his intelligence. As he himself put it: ''After suffering manifold perils and hardships, peace of mind at last returned to me, and I decided that I must bid farewell to politics for good. I therefore decided to write accounts of some episodes in Roman history that seemed particularly worthy of record.''

His works were hugely popular due to his style, the dramatic way he staged his subjects, his willingness to describe the depravity of others and, forgetting his own disreputable actions, he assured the reader they got their comeuppance [a little like the pot calling the kettle black]. The problem for us, one that will remain unresolved, is to distinguish fact from exaggeration, and given Sallust's background, to what extent Sallust went to avenge himself on those he didn't particularly care for, the most important of whom was Catiline himself. I'll relate what he wrote, and always name him as the source, as well as the observations of historians who disagree with Sallust. From a distance of 2000-plus years there's nothing more I can offer in the way of searching out the truth.

The introduction of Sallust's book on Catiline is so perfect, so in line with what I believe, that I'm going to reproduce it in it entirety, the translation of Sallust's *The Conspiracy of Catiline* by S.A. Handford [1898-1978]: ''Every man who wishes to rise superior to the lower animals should strive his hardest to avoid living all his days in silent obscurity, like the beasts of the field, creatures which go with their faces to the ground and are the slaves of their bellies. We human beings have mental as well as physical powers; the mind, which we share with gods, is the ruling element in us, while the chief function of the body, which we have in common with the beasts, is to obey. Surely, therefore, it is our intellectual rather than our physical powers that we should use in the pursuit of fame. Since only a short span of life has been vouchsafed us, we must make ourselves remembered as long as may be by those who come after us. Wealth and beauty can give only a fleeting and perishable fame, but intellectual excellence is a glorious and everlasting possession.''

Sallust fully believed in the Trojan War [as do I] and the founding of Rome by Aeneas [ditto].

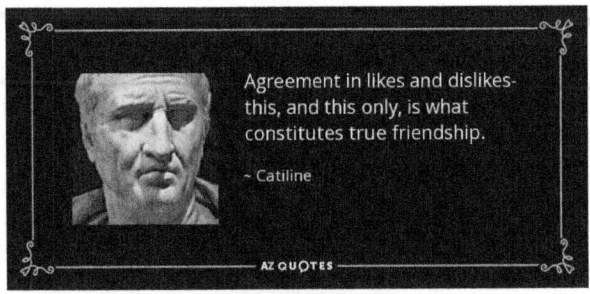

Agreement in likes and dislikes-
this, and this only, is what
constitutes true friendship.

~ Catiline

AZ QUOTES

Catiline.

Catiline had been elected quaestor in 74 B.C at age 30 [a quaestor supervised the treasury and conducted audits], aedile in 70 B.C. [responsible for the maintenance of buildings and the regulation of festivals] and praetor in 68 B.C. [judicial responsibilities]. These offices gave him membership in the Senate. Charismatic and attractive, his having served under Sulla, and his backing of the dictator, enhanced his reputation. Crassus at first bankrolled him, followed by Caesar who, attracted by the force of his character and his ambition, also gave him money, probably Crassus', as Caesar owned him 25 million sesterces [at a ballpark $1.50 per sesterce].

THE FIRST CONSPIRACY

66 B.C.

Catiline was governor in Africa in 67 and 66 B.C., returning to Rome to run for Consul. But a delegation from Africa accused him of financial abuses, which was sufficient to prevent his becoming a candidate, although he was later found innocent.

The First Conspiracy was therefore aimed at seizing power by other means, in this case through the murder of the Consuls and certain senators, although Sallust is the unique historian who mentioned the Conspiracy, which he covered in his book in only a score of words, the reason that some historians refute its ever having taken place.

65 B.C.

In 65 B.C. Cato the Younger [Marcus Porcius Cato Uticensis] brought him to trial, accused, along with other men, of playing roles in Sullan proscription, Catiline indicted for the murder of his brother-in-law Marcus Gratidianus, whose head he publicly cut off and carried through the streets of Rome, his intimacy with Sulla such that he persuaded the dictator to add Gratidianus' name to his list of proscriptions, thusly legalizing the crime. Caesar, a friend of Catiline's at the time, presided over the court before which Cato sought justice, and was therefore able to see that Catiline got off scot-free.

THE SECOND CONSPIRACY

64 B.C.

In 64 B.C. Catiline was allowed to run for Consul in the 63 elections, backed by many men of renown, including two sons of Sulla, perhaps even Crassus who welcomed a man of power who could threaten that of Pompey, Crassus' chief rival. Despite his wealth, Crassus was a man who lacked luck. He had won the war against Spartacus, but Pompey, at only age 24, had been given credit. He thusly attempted to gain Pompey's allegiance by buying up land that he would turn over to him for his retiring troops, but this was foiled by Cicero on the Senate floor. He loaned money to Caesar, making it clear that he would never be called to repay it, but Caesar nonetheless drew so close to Pompey that he offered Pompey his daughter in marriage. He set off to conquer Parthia but lost battle after battle, finally suing for peace when his dear son was killed. Fearing a trap, his men tried to dissuade him from leaving camp and a tug-a-war ensued between them and Parthians set on his accompanying them, which resulted in his death and the slaughter of his men. His head was cut off and delivered to the Parthian king during the staging of a play, that the king gave to the actors to use as a prop. Its mouth was later filled with molten gold in punishment for his known greed and, according to Plutarch, a captured soldier who resembled him was dressed as a woman and paraded around the court, to the glee of all except the impersonator.

Cicero had also considered joining forces with Catiline, in return for Catiline's help with Cicero's candidacy, as two Consuls were elected each year. At the time, Cicero described Catiline as ''a strong mixture of evil and good, a man of enormous energy, a brave soldier, popular with a wide circle of friends to whom he was intensely loyal, generous with both his money and with his time.''

In addition to these men, Catiline enlisted a huge number of Roman youths, boys born with a silver spoon in their mouths, idle boys bored with having everything at their fingertips, whom Catiline could offer adventure and positions of power that was out of their reach because they lacked the energy and ambition to search it out in the traditional way, by drumming up the support of voters, boys with whom he was accused of unspeakable profligacies. Catiline had vitality and ambition in unlimited quantity, he knew how to flatter and wind the boys around his little finger, how to use their wealth and benefit from the prestige linked to their families. Not only was the *jeunesse dorée* of Rome attracted to Catiline, but Sallust states that the city had become the home of all those lost in vice and disgraceful excesses, who poured in until ''Rome was like a sewer.'' Sallust continued: ''Many, remembering Sulla's victory, and seeing men who had served under him as common soldiers now risen to be senators, or so rich that they lived as luxuriously as kings, began to hope that they too, if they took up arms, might find victory a source of profit. Young men from the country, whose labor on the farms had barely kept them from starvation, had been attracted by the private and public doles available at Rome, and preferred an idle city life to such thankless toil. These, like all the rest, stood to gain by public calamities. It is no wonder, therefore, that these paupers, devoid of moral scruple and incited by ambitious hopes, should have held their country as cheap as they held themselves. Those also to whom Sulla's victory had brought disaster by the proscription of their parents, the confiscation of their property, and the curtailment of their civil rights, looked forward with no less sanguine expectations to what might result from the coming struggle.''

This is an additional reminder that the root of evil that eventually destroyed Rome's Republic, sending the city on a course of utter disaster, was Sulla.

To them were added thousands of Italians, spread throughout Italy in colonies, set up by previous governments to occupy and secure the lands, as well as soldiers given land for their retirement, men especially loyal to the memory of Sulla, whom Catiline had fought alongside, and whose sons, as said, backed Catiline. They all possessed citizenship and so had voting rights, although they would have to make their way to Rome to cast their ballot, a huge handicap, largely the reason Catiline lost the election. Catiline then billed himself the champion of the poor, the bankrupt and the dispossessed, offering all a populist *tabula novae*, a clean slate and his Plan B, revolt. Concerning the Senate, Catiline compared it to the people, stating they were ''two bodies, one frail and sickly with an empty head, the other strong and healthy, but headless.'' Catiline had every intention of becoming that head.

In a meeting at the home of Marcus Porcius Laeca, Catiline told his supporters that they had been chosen as his companions because they were courageous and loyal, and all shared the same likes and dislikes, ''the solid foundation of friendship.'' Without power they were nobodies, he told them, subservient to those with authority and wealth. Better to die and have done with it rather than live on in poverty and dishonor. ''We have the strength of youth and stout hearts'', he continued, ''not enfeebled by age and soft living.'' Catiline placed himself in the service of his men, telling them to use him ''as a soldier or as your commander: my heart and my hands shall be at your service.''

He went on to promise them the cancellation of their debts and the proscription of the rich [declaring them enemies of the Republic, which allows men in power to kill them and take their fortunes, homes and land]. He assured them that armies would back him once he was elected Consul, naming Piso's troops in Spain and Publius Sittius' men near Salerno, to the south of Rome. At the end of the speech he ''called on them to swear an oath, and passed around bowls of human blood mixed with wine, invoking a curse on them all if they broke faith,'' writes Sallust.

Among them was Quintus Curius, a man of good birth but so tainted by vice and crime that the Senate had expulsed him for immoral conduct [that Sallust, alas, doesn't clarify]. Curius had a mistress, Fulvia, of immense importance because she would repeatedly warn Cicero, through people they had in common, of impending dangers, without ever revealing the name of Curius. She had come to the conclusion that Curius was dangerous to her, as well as the Republic, when he threatened to stab her to death if she didn't comply with his demands, while promising her wealth if she did. [While Sallust maintains that it was Curius himself who sent out the warnings.]

Cicero spread word of Catiline's plans to kill senators and other wealthy nobles through prescription. Sallust claimed that it was due to fear that Catiline would carry out his threats that convinced the electorate to choose Cicero, an Optimate, and Gaius Antonius, a Populares, as Consuls, Antonius who was the uncle of Mark Antony and an intimate friend of Catiline's [although perhaps in secret, as few people wanted their names connected to his infamous reputation]. Antonius was in desperate financial straits and would have much preferred the election of Catiline, if only for the money from the proscriptions that would save him from debt. Later, Mark Antony, along with Octavian, the future Emperor Augustus, would be responsible for the deaths of hundreds through proscriptions, including Cicero, as related in the chapter on Caesar. In the 63 election Crassus and Caesar had splurged so much money that the Senate decided to limit campaign spending, the first time in history. Cicero gave such an impassioned speech it its favor that, even though it was voted down, it made him extremely popular in the Senate and in the people's eyes.

Antonius, his full name Gaius Antonius Hybrida, earned his name Hybrida, meaning half-beast, when Sulla put him in control of Greece in order to maintain peace there. Instead, he plundered and killed the people under him. Antonius was purged from the Senate several times, but always succeeded in making a comeback, in one case thanks to Mark Antony who took one of Antonius' daughters for his second wife, and on another occasion Antony wanted him back in Rome because Antonius owned him money.

Cicero's early support of a murderer and thug like Antonius is proof that Cicero was not as squeaky-clean as he would have Romans believe.

Catiline's loss of the consulship only served to spur him on, to seek money from followers that he used to raise men for an army and buy weapons to arm them. His promise to cancel debts, and obtain wealth by killing those who had it, attracted more and more supporters, as did his promise to extend citizenship to all Italians. Sallust notes that even prostitutes, fallen on bad times because they had lost their looks, joined his ranks, women Catiline sent to enlist the help of slaves and to ''organize acts of incendiarism'', even apparently promising to assure their heritage by murdering their husbands, should the women so wish. One of the women was Sempronia, that Sallust claims had wit and charm, knew Greek and Latin literature, could dance and play the lyre, her passions so ardent that she made advances on men, generously showering them with money, but was also a perjurer, a liar and an ''accessary to murder'', states Sallust, without, alas, going into detail. Modern feminists suggest that she was the precursor of today's Italian women, in her search of learning and the disposal of her body as she thought fit. Besides her role in the Second Conspiracy, she was the mother of Decimus Junius Brutus Albinus who, along with Marcus Junius Brutus and others, murdered Caesar.

Caesar too had apparently backed Catiline during the earlier stages of his career, as reported, Caesar who knew how to recognize men of exceptional ability, men whose charism, like Catiline's, was easy to succumb to.

18 October

On October the 18th Cicero was roused from his bed by Crassus, accompanied by two patricians, Marcus Marcellus and Metellus Scipio. Crassus had a letter he'd just received, warning him of an impending massacre and urging him to flee Rome, a letter received by other men of importance, most of whom were senators, warning them too to leave the capital or face assassination. Cicero and Crassus believed the letters had been sent by Caelius, a friend of both men, as well as an intimate of Catiline. [Six years later, in 57 B.C., Caelius was successfully defended in court by both Crassus and Cicero when accused of murder by a jealous mistress. Later still he sided with Caesar against Pompey in their fratricidal war, but then turned against Caesar when Caesar didn't back his proposal for debt relief, which sparked a rebellion during which Caelius was killed.]

19 October

Cicero convened the Senate and read out the letter. The Consuls, of which Cicero was one, were instructed to make inquiries. Many in the Senate refused to believe that such a conspiracy was undergoing, especially by someone lacking in troops like Catiline, and although they were aware of his ability to charm wayward aristocratic youths, and his appeal to the poor and landless, they felt him incapable of a mass uprising, and certainly not the assassination of themselves, a body into which Catiline so desired to enter. ''Cicero was accused of creating an atmosphere of fear,'' summed up Sallust, in part because every senator had a son, nephew or cousin who had joined Catiline. Catiline instructed the Tribune Lucius Bestia to wait until the people truly doubted Cicero, and then go before the Senate and inform them that Cicero was inventing the entire conspiracy in order for the Senate to give him dictatorial powers. This would be the signal for an uprising, and already men and arms had been dispersed throughout Rome, to be used to kill the oligarchy of patricians that had ruled the city since being installed by Sulla. Sons who had joined Catiline, most underage and from noble families, had been instructed by Catiline to kill their fathers. They would then, amidst the bloodshed and burning of the Forum, ride off to join Manlius' forces [Manlius will be introduced in a moment]. The final act of the uprising would see Catiline declared dictator [protector of the people].

20 October

Quintus Arrius, a former general who had lost a battle against Spartacus, brought information concerning events in Etruria, where Catiline could find help among the people reduced to poverty, ripe for revolt since Sulla deprived them of lands and possessions, followed by Roman taxes and indebtedness that touched even the retired legions there, people who were tired of the corruption of the magistrates, men for whom they were nothing more than provincial cows to be milked dry.

Sallust had no sympathy for those forced to revolt, as he states in this excerpt from his book: "In spite of two senatorial decrees, not one man among all the conspirators was induced by the promise of reward to betray their plans, and not one deserted from Catiline's camp. A deadly moral contagion had infected all their minds. And this madness was not confined to those actually implicated in the plot. The whole of the lower orders, impatient for a new regime, looked with favor on Catiline's enterprise. In this they only did what might have been expected of them. In every country paupers envy respectable citizens and make heroes of unprincipled characters, hating the established order of things and hankering after innovation; discontented with their own lot, they are bent on general upheaval. Turmoil and rebellion bring them carefree profit, since poverty has nothing to lose." Sallust's distaste for Catiline and his followers could not have *not* influenced his history of Catiline.

21 October

Cicero convened the Senate that passed the *Senatus Consultum Ultimum,* a hugely powerful decree that gave a Consul dictatorial powers for the purpose of "preserving the state", after Cicero [who as Consul was now in possession of said dictatorial powers] informed the Senate that Catiline's head of troops, Caius Manlius, a former Sullan centurion, would take up arms on the 27th of October, and that a massacre of Catiline's enemies was planned for the 28th, after which, on 1 November, Praeneste, a stronghold just north of Rome, would be seized. The information may have come from Arrius or another source, but Sallust believed that the person responsible for the disclosures was

Fulvia, mistress, as said, of Quintus Curius. Curius had fallen into debt, one of the reasons he backed Catiline who had promised that not only would debts be written off, but money would be taken from the wealthy through proscriptions in order to restore the fortunes of those like Curius. Fulvia had decided to leave him in search of greener pastures, and to keep her Curius had disclosed Catiline's plans for revolt. Perhaps in order to play both sides of the field, Fulvia went to Cicero's wife Terentia to whom she leaked everything.

Senator Lucius Saenius read out a letter from Fiesole in Etruria [today's Tuscany] stating that Manlius had taken to the field at the head of a huge army. Other senators reported evil portents and omens, amidst rumors of plotters' meetings and arms transported from place to place. Word seeped out to the people, now rife with despondency and fear, praying for aid from heaven. One aristocratic boy left to join Malius' forces. He ''was dragged back when already on his way and put to death on his father's command,'' wrote Sallust.

Cicero secured the capital with forces and dispatched troops to reinforce Praeneste. When news was received that slaves in Capua and Apulia were in revolt, Quintus Marcius Rex and Quintus Metellus Creticus were sent to deal with Apulia, Quintus Ruffus and Quintus Metellus Celer made for Capua, accompanied by gladiators. Rex's mission involved his keeping a close eye on Manlius and his troops. When Manlius found out, he sent a letter to Rex, stating that he didn't wish to rise up against Rome, but that debt had reduced him and his followers to wretched poverty and loss of reputation. He begged the Senate to allow the common people to pay their outstanding debts in copper and not silver, which had been permitted in earlier times [a scaling down of debts by 75%]. ''We do not seek power but only to live as free human beings.'' He beseeched the Senate to rescue him and his fellow citizens, to restore their liberties, and ''not force us to seek a means of selling our life's blood as dearly as we can'', a direct reference to war.

Rex answered by telling Manlius to go before the Senate, where he would certainly be shown clemency and compassion. But his reply arrived too late, by then the Senate had declared both

Catiline and Manlius public enemies, although it again offered pardons to their followers if they immediately laid down their arms.

6 November

Catiline planned to soon leave Rome and take control of his troops himself, presently under Manlius near Fiesole in Etruria, and then proceed to Picenum and Cisalpine Gaul [see following map--2 December] to take command of troops there, which Catiline's enemies referred to as being nothing more than mobs armed with just sharpened stakes [which many of the poor were]. He met with other conspirators at a location in Rome where they planned to set the city on fire and assassinate Cicero.

7 November

Gaius Cornelius and Lucius Vargunteius went to Cicero's home, but Cicero had been warned by Fulvia. He fled, after installing men there as guards, which dissuaded the assassins from even trying to enter.

8 November

Cicero convened the Senate in the Temple of Jupiter Stator at the foot of the Palatine Hill, the building surrounded by armed knights. Incredibly, Catiline took his seat. He was immediately isolated by senators who moved more or less surreptitiously away, as seen on the jacket of this book. Cicero gave his First Speech Against Catiline. Cicero began by shouting out the words, *Quo usque tandem abutere, Catilina, patientia nostra? Quam diu etiam furor iste tuus nos eludet? Quem ad finem sese effrenata iactabit audacia?* ''When, O Catiline, do you mean to cease abusing our patience? How long is that madness of yours still to mock us? When is there to be an end of that unbridled audacity of yours, swaggering about as it does now?'', to which he added, *O tempora, o mores!* ''Oh, what time! Oh, what behavior!'' After which

Catiline rose to rebut, assuring the Senate that he and his family had served Rome for generations, and it was certainly not now that he would initiate any form of revolt. Then, turning to face Cicero, he asked the senators how they could believe ''a mere immigrant?''

Shouted down by the senators who cried out ''Traitor! Enemy! Child murderer!'', Catiline left the temple, hurling ''If you try to set a fire against me, I won't fight it with water, but with destruction!'' and went home where he told his followers to go ahead with the burning of Rome, during which time he would ride off to join the troops headed by Manlius. He nonetheless took a moment to write certain senators, telling them he had decided to voluntarily exile himself to Massilia [Marseille], the traditional form of retreat chosen by patricians found guilty of crimes. This, wrote Catiline, was to avoid the horrors of a civil war, Catiline's attempt to lower their guard, the ultimate form of deception and betrayal.

Catiline was still to be found in Rome, apparently serene, when Lucius Aemilous Paulus threatened to prosecute him for treason. Catiline volunteered to place himself in the hands of Cicero or other nobles designated by the Senate, but Cicero refused to go ahead with any move against Catiline until he had iron proof of the plot and Catiline's role in the affair. In order to obtain it, rewards of 100,000 sesterces and freedom were offered to slaves for information about the conspiracy, 200,000 to citizens, plus a full pardon should they have taken part in the conspiracy.

The offers brought forth not a single traitor to Catiline's cause.

Temple of Jupiter Stator

9 November

Cicero went to the Forum where he gave his Second Speech Against Catiline, his audience senators and the people. He accused Catiline of getting support from five classes of men. The first were men who had possessions but also great debts that they hoped Catiline would abolish. The second class had debts but their desire was ''supreme power. They wished to become masters. They think that when the Republic is in confusion they may gain those honors which they despair of when it is in tranquility.'' The third class ''already touched by age, but still vigorous from constant exercise, of which class is Manlius himself.'' Under Sulla they had had sudden wealth, had had farms, litters, vast numbers of slaves, but now ''incurred such great debts that, if they would be saved, they must raise Sulla from the dead'', or have Catiline rescue them. The forth class ''are lazy insolvents'' who want Catiline to help them ''with embarrassing old debts''. The final class are the boys who care for their hair and trim their beards, who party till daybreak, gamble and dance naked at feasts, Catiline's ''bodyguard of prostitutes''. In this speech Cicero told Romans they had nothing to fear, as they had Cicero as their Consul and the support of the gods. He told them that Catiline had left the city, accompanied by men in debt, men eager for power and wealth, many of whom were Sulla's veterans, ruined men who had turned to crime. The speech was apparently aimed at the lower classes, who were told that if they followed Catiline they too would be ruined, while Cicero would care for their needs should they continue to put their trust in him.

17 November

News reached Rome that Catiline had made it to the camp of Manlius, leaving Rome in the hands of Publius Cornelius Lentulus. Both Catiline and Manlius were declared public enemies and the Consuls were instructed to raise troops. Antonius was dispatched to pursue Catiline while Cicero remained in Rome to defend the capital. Amnestry was again offered the conspirators, but again there wasn't a single defector.

Catiline had the possibility of taking on slaves that Sallust wrote flocked to him. But he refused their help for fear of what Romans would say to his taking on runaways, upon whom Roman households were founded, slaves who did everything from wipe their asses to instruct their children, as many were far better educated than their masters, especially captured Greeks. And they provided sexual relief, Romans who could choose between girls and boys, unmarried women from the best hung, as it was often *that*, as well as their strength and their teeth, the chief selling point.

Of the conspirators still in Rome, Gaius Cethegus wanted to put into effect, immediately, the plans to kill Cicero, burn the city and occupy strategic points, but he was overruled by Lentulus who ordered it done at a later date, possibly around mid-December. Lentulus claimed that it had been prophesied in the Sibylline Books that he was destined to rule Rome, the certainly of which turned him traitor. [The Sibylline Books were written by Greek oracles [Sibyls] that predicted events that would take place during the Republic and the Empire--a bit like our reference to Nostradamus; the books were later deliberately destroyed so as not to fall into the wrong hands]. In the meantime, he had the Tribune Lucius Calpurnius Bestia go before the senators and proclaim that Cicero was responsible for the present mayhem by accusing innocent men of revolt, Cicero's aim being to provoke a war and install himself as permanent dictator. Later in the day the conspirators agreed that Rome would be burned on 17 December, during the Saturnalia, a festival of pagan origin when a public banquet was offered to the people and masters served their slaves food and wine. Gag gifts were exchanged, a King of Saturnalia chosen, gambling was allowed and in more ancient times men dressed as women, women as men [and in still earlier Greek times there were human sacrifices], that the poet Catullus described as the best of all festivals, perhaps in part because both men and women were encouraged to freely share their bodies. The mayhem would be a perfect setting for a bonfire enveloping all of

Rome. Cicero and other leaders would not be forgotten, for it was during the festivities that they were to be murdered.

2 December

Lentulus learned that a delegation from the Allobrogue had arrived in Italy from Transalpine Gaul [between today's Lyons and Geneva] to request redress from the Senate for Roman misrule and financial malfeasance, as well as relief from the burden of the taxes Rome imposed on them. Caesar had fought the Allobrogues and had declared that they were "outstandingly courageous", a people who didn't hesitate to fight against Romans, as they had fought against Hannibal when he dared enter their territory. One of Spartacus' lieutenants, Crixus, had been an Allobragian Gaul, all reasons why Lentulus was eager to have them on Catiline's side. Lentulus sent word to the delegation that Catiline was willing to assuage Allobrogue grievances if the Allobroges backed the conspiracy. Publius Gabinius Capito headed the discussions, but he proved so unconvincing that the Allobroges went to Quintus Fabius Sanga, a patrician and friend of Cicero, with the details of the plot. Cicero, through Sanga, instructed the Allobroges to continue the talks, going so far as to oblige the ringleaders to sign a document promising that Catiline would redress their grievances in exchange for Allobroge aid. Lentulus, Cethegus and Statilius signed the agreement, but not the fourth major conspirator, Cassius who, sensing that something was wrong, planned to leave Rome and join Catiline's troops.

The evening of 2 December the Allobroges left Rome with the documents in hand, accompanied by a Catiline supporter, Titus Volturcius, and headed for their homeland where they would raise troops for Catiline.

Cicero, more in charge than ever, gave troops to Lucius Vaterius Flaccus and Gaius Pomptinus with orders to arrest the traitors at the Mulvian Bridge on the Via Flaminia, where it crossed the Tiber, two miles north of Rome.

During his absence the home of Gaius Cethegus was rifled, and spears, knives and swords found. Theatrically, Cicero had them brought to the Senate and cast on the floor before the wide-eyed senators [just as Hannibal had had his brother Mago empty a sack, over the Carthaginian Council floor, containing the thousands of rings taken from the dead bodies of Romans, deeply shocking the Council, after the slaughter at Cannae.].

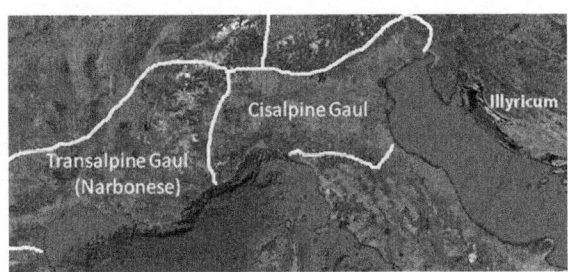

The Allobroges' Transalpine Gaul and Catiline's destination, Cisalpine Gaul.

3 December

The Gauls and the dissidents reached the bridge on 3 December and, after a scuffle, surrendered. They were taken prisoner to the Temple of Concord where they faced the Senate, the temple packed, the temple grounds securely in the hands of Cicero's armed guards.

Volturicus was questioned first. He at first pleaded innocence but then accepted full immunity in exchange for a detailed account of the conspiracy. The Allobroges came next, confirming Volturicus' version and seconding Volturicus' testimony against Lentulus, Cethegus, Statilius and Gabinius. When confronted with the documents they had signed, the four confessed, thanks to which other conspirators were arrested, among them Cassius who had fled Rome but had not reached Gaul as he'd planned.

The men were put in custody at the homes of prominent senators, as the prison in Rome was too rudimentary and filthy for men of their standing. Cicero was awarded a senatorial thanksgiving for having saved the country. He went to the Forum where he gave his Third Speech Against Catiline, informing the people of what had transpired in the Senate and the events leading up to the capture of the prisoners. He told them they should rejoice because they had been saved from a bloody rebellion, and that the victory had been more difficult than in foreign lands because the enemies were Romans.

Temple of Concord

4 December

On the 4th of December two strange plots evolved, which implicated both Crassus and Caesar in the conspiracy. Lucius Tarquinius came before the Senate and testified, in exchange for a pardon, that he had been sent, by Crassus, to warn Catiline that no matter what he heard was going on in Rome, he was to march into the city and massacre all those who would not come over to Cataline's side, as well as free the men the Senate had imprisoned. The testimony caused a huge upheaval, due to Crassus' wealth and influence. Many of the senators received or had received money from Crassus, that they wished kept secret, others were in business with him or in his debt in one way or another. This may have been the case with Cicero too, because he immediately muzzled Tarquinius, putting him away out of the sight and hearing of senators who had not participated in his questioning. Tarquinius was finally accused of inventing the whole story [his final destiny unknown to us].

As for Caesar, Quintus Catulus and Gaius Piso used forged evidence to implicate him in the conspiracy, evidence not believed although neither man was arrested. As for their reasons: Catulus' hatred for Caesar dated from the time when they were rivals for the same office, which Caesar won, and Caesar had accused Piso of embezzling funds from the Allobroges, one of the motivations for their descent to Rome. Most historians agree that Piso was a thoroughly dishonest rascal.

Then Cicero received news that an attempt would be made to liberate the ringleaders, purportedly led by the freedmen and slaves of Lentulus and Cethegus. In response he doubled their guard.

5 December

The next day, the 5th of December, was crucially important for the leaders of the conspiracy. The Senate met in the Temple of Concord. The temple, the Forum and all approaches were quarantined. Although Cicero now possessed all authority, he nonetheless sought the consent of the Senate for his proposition, brought to the Senate floor by Cicero's handpicked first speaker, the consul-elect Junius Silanus, who moved that the men under custody, along with Lucius Longius, Publius Furius and the brothers Umbrenus and Quintus Annius, be put to death. Fellow consul-elect Lucius Morena, as well as 14 other past Consuls, seconded the motion, the whole transcribed by Marcus Tiro, Cicero's freed slave and the inventor of shorthand, who published Cicero's works and a biography of his master after Cicero's death, following him at age 99. Cicero knew that Caesar was against the death penalty, as related in Suetonius' *The Twelve Caesars*, but for the sake of equanimity asked him to present his views. Caesar's concern was for the precedent that would be set if the men were killed without trial, something the Senate had no right to do as it had no judicial powers under the Constitution [the same reason evoked by Elizabeth I a millennium and a half later when she hesitated to have Mary Queen of Scots decapitated, a precedent which could someday apply to Elizabeth herself, she felt, and indeed Charles I was later beheaded]. Perhaps Caesar feared for himself or those of his family, in a Rome deprived of the rule of law. As there were no jails as such in Rome, Caesar suggested that the conspirators be parceled out to the major provinces, where they would be under the house arrest of governors, which would have made escape relatively easy should a plotter decide to take that path. To allay fears, Caesar proposed that the Senate pass a law forbidding the murder of senators, a law the Senate had no authority to pass and no way of enforcing. But basically, the suggestion of house arrest was more contrary to Roman *tradition* than was outright executions.

Cicero then gave Cato the floor, who pleaded for the death penalty, stating that Caesar's suggestion of arrest was not only unworkable, but that such light punishment would be an encouragement to all men who wished to overthrow the government and kill senators and Consuls in their beds [and, of course, should one of the men double back to Rome, Cicero would have been the first on his list]. Cato regained his seat to great applause.

Cicero rose and summarized the views of all concerned. He had to be subtle, because a Consul didn't have the right to choose sides in the debates before the Senate, and at the opening of the session Cicero knew that the vast majority of senators was against the death penalty. He thusly had to be evenhanded, while somehow indicating that the way to light and salvation lay through Cato's reasoning, not Caesar's.

He then requested a vote, the huge majority deciding in favor of death, even Catiline's friend Catulus, that Catiline had helped murder Gratidianus, breaking his body and slitting his throat over the grave of Catulus' father.

No time was wasted due, perhaps, to the fear of an armed intervention by men Catiline may have quartered in the city. The conspirators, Publius Cornelius Lentulus, Lucius Statilius, Publius Gabinius and Marcus Caeparius, were taken to the Tullianum prison and strangled with a noose.

When Cicero exited he said, *Vixere*! "They have lived!".

On his way home he was hailed by the people as their savior. Amusingly, Sallust adds that what turned the people in Cicero's favor was the discloser that Rome would have been burned to the ground, with the loss of their property, down to their clothes. Otherwise, he states, they would have welcomed revolt as a way of enriching themselves through plunder.

The Tullianum, described as dark and foul smelling.
It was originally a cistern, constructed 600 years earlier, where prisoners were kept in an upper chamber or lowered through an opening into a dungeon, a system that still existed into the Renaissance in Venice. Its name may have come from tullius, a jet of water [referring to its use as a cistern], although an alternative origin is the name of one of the earlier kings, Tullus Hostilius or Servius Tullius. Imprisonment as such was rare, the Tullianum being basically a holding cell. Otherwise, patricians were allowed exile [plus fines, confiscation of property and loss of citizen rights], while slaves and lower-status citizens were sentenced to hard labor on ships or in mills and mines, or simply executed. One could be incarcerated for debt, as in later London.

The lower chamber was circular and cut in the rock, its entry at the top through a 28-inch [70-centimeter] hole. Prisoners were lowered 6 feet [2 meters] to the ground by ropes, or simply thrown in. It was in the lower chamber that, according to Sallust, the conspirators were throttled. [The apostles Peter and Paul were held there.]

10 December

On the 10th of December Quintus Nepos declared, in a meeting open to the people, that the execution of citizens without trial was unacceptable, and that Cicero should no longer be allowed to speak in public.

3 January

The Senate passed a resolution, aimed at undermining Nepos, stating that all men who had had a part in the condemnation of the traitors be given full immunity.

Cataline's Camp

The executions in Rome caused 3/4^{ths} of Catiline's 20,000 troops to desert, as most were there in anticipation of the gold in the Roman treasury, the Aerarium, their booty once the city capitulated to Catiline's armies [later Pompey would flee Rome, leaving the treasury to Caesar whose first move was to axe down the doors--see Caesar's chapter].

What remained of Catiline's forces set out for Transalpine Gaul but came upon the legions headed by Quintus Metellus and Antonius near Pistoria. At first Catiline hoped to escape through side-roads to Gaul, but he was cut off, thanks to men sent out to track his army, and inhabitants that could win favors or quick cash by signaling Catiline's whereabouts. Because Antonius was considered a friend, Catiline headed in his direction in the hope of an easier fight. Antonius, learning of Catiline's approach and guessing the reason, developed an opportune illness. He turned over command of his legions to his aid, Marcus Petreius, a man of great experience.

Despite the urgency, Catiline took the time to write a letter to Catulus, who had voted in favor of his death, defending himself by explaining that he had taken up the cause of the wretched poor because he too had suffered from insults and injuries, denied the offices that would have recognized his work and restored him and his family to a position of honor. His only alternative would be an honorable death, and he ended by begging Catulus to care for his wife Orestilla.

Catiline addressed his men: ''I counsel you to be brave and resolute, and when you go into battle to remember that riches, honor, glory and, what is more, your liberty and the future of your country, lie in your hands. If we win we shall be sure of getting all we want: we shall have plenty of supplies and all the towns will open their gates. For us, country, freedom, and life are at stake; they, on the other hand, have no particular interest in fighting to keep an oligarchy in power. Let these thoughts, and the memory of your past valor, inspire you to attack them with all the greater boldness. In battle it is always the greatest cowards who are in the greatest danger; courage is like a wall of defense. But if, in spite of this, Fortune robs your valor of its just reward, see that you do not sell your lives cheaply. Do not be taken and slaughtered like cattle. Fight like men: let bloodshed and mourning be the price that the enemy will have paid for his victory.'' Catiline carried the standard of an eagle, the very same standard Marius, who had also fought for the rights of Italics, had carried aloft through his campaigns [when the Senate found out, they deprived Catiline of his Roman citizenship].

The fighting was bitter, often in close quarters with daggers, and Manlius was among the first killed. Seeing that the end was near, Catiline threw himself into the center of the fray. Just as no man had turned traitor against Catiline and accepted amnesty [other than Volturicus], so now too did his men fight to the finish, even the wounded who left their beds to die at the side of their leader and companions.

As for Cicero, he always considered the destruction of Catiline, dead at age 46, his life's greatest achievement.

As the dead on both sides had been ''friends, relatives or men who had been their guests or hosts,'' states Sallust, ''gladness and rejoicing were tempered by grief and lamentation.''

With these words, Sallust concludes his book.

~~~~~~

APPENDIX A

CICERO'S ORATIONS AGAINST CATILINE

CICERO'S FIRST ORATION AGAINST CATILINE

Translated by C.D. Yonge, slightly abridged

When, O Catiline, do you mean to cease abusing our patience? How long is that madness of yours still to mock us? When is there to be an end of that unbridled audacity of yours, swaggering about as it does now? Do you not feel that your plans are detected? Do you not see that your conspiracy is already arrested and rendered powerless by the knowledge which everyone here possesses of it?

The Senate is aware of these things; the Consul sees them; and yet this man lives. Lives! aye, he comes even into the Senate. He takes a part in the public deliberations; he is watching and marking down and checking off for slaughter every individual among us. And we, gallant men that we are, think that we are doing our duty to the Republic if we keep out of the way of his frenzied attacks.

You ought, O Catiline, long ago to have been led to execution by command of the Consul. That destruction which you have been long plotting against us ought to have already fallen on your own head.

What? Did not that most illustrious man, Publius Scipio, the Pontifex Maximus, in his capacity of a private citizen, put to death Tiberius Gracchus, though but slightly undermining the Constitution? And shall we, who are the Consuls, tolerate Catiline, openly desirous to destroy the whole world with fire and slaughter? There was--there was once such virtue in this Republic, that brave men would repress mischievous citizens with severer chastisement than the most bitter enemy. For we have a resolution of the Senate, a formidable and authoritative decree against you, O Catiline; the wisdom of the Republic is not at fault, nor the dignity of this senatorial body. We, we alone--I say it openly--we, the consuls, are waiting in our duty.

CICERO'S SECOND ORATION AGAINST CATILINE

Translated by C.D. Yonge, slightly abridged

At length, O Romans, we have dismissed from the city, or driven out, or, when he was departing of his own accord, we have pursued with words, Lucius Catiline, mad with audacity, breathing wickedness, impiously planning mischief to his country, threatening fire and sword to you and to this city. He is gone, he has departed, he has disappeared, he has rushed out. No injury will now be prepared against these walls within the walls themselves by that monster and prodigy of wickedness. And we have, without controversy, defeated him, the sole general of this domestic war. For now that dagger will no longer hover about our sides; we shall not be afraid in the campus, in the Forum, in the senate-house and within our own private walls, he was moved from his place when he was driven from the city. Now we shall openly carry on a regular war with an enemy without hindrance. Beyond all question we ruin the man; we have defeated him splendidly when we have driven him from secret treachery into open warfare. But that he has not taken with him his sword red with blood as he intruded, that he has left us alive, that we wrested the weapon from his hands, that he has left the citizens safe and the city standing, what great and overwhelming grief must you think that this is to him. Now he lies prostrate, O Romans, and feels himself stricken down and abject, and often casts back his eyes towards this city, which he mourns over as snatched from his jaws, but which seems to me to rejoice at having vomited forth such a pest, and cast it out of doors.

But if there be any one of that disposition which all men should have, who yet blames me greatly for the very thing in which my speech exults and triumphs--namely, that I did not arrest so capital mortal an enemy rather than let him go--that is not my fault, O citizens, but the fault of the times. Lucius Catiline ought to have been visited with the severest punishment, and to have been put to death long since; and both the customs of our ancestors, and the rigor of my office, and the Republic, demanded this of me; but how many, think you, were there who did not believe what I reported? How many who out of stupidity did not think so? How many who even defended him? How many who, out of their own depravity, favored him? If, in truth, I had thought that, if he were removed, all danger would he removed from you, I would long since have cut off Lucius Catiline, had it been at the risk, not only of my popularity, but even of my life.

But as I saw that, since the matter was not even then proved to all of you, if I had punished him with death, as he had deserved, I should be borne down by unpopularity, and so be unable to follow up his accomplices, I brought the business on to this point that you might be able to combat openly when you saw the enemy without disguise. But how exceedingly I think this enemy to be feared now that he is out of doors, you may see from this--that I am vexed even that he has gone from the city with but a small retinue. I wish he had taken with him all his forces. He has taken with him Tongillus, with whom he had been said to have a criminal intimacy, and Publicius, and Munatius, whose debts contracted in taverns could cause no great disquietude to the Republic. He has left behind him others--you all know what men they are, how overwhelmed with debt, how powerful, how noble.

I thoroughly despise his army composed of desperate old men, of clownish profligates, and uneducated spendthrifts. I wish he had taken with him those soldiers of his, whom I see hovering about the forum, standing about the senate-house, even coming into the Senate, who shine with ointment, who glitter in purple; and if they remain here, remember that that army is not so much to be feared by us as these men who have deserted the army. And they are the more to be feared, because they are aware that I know what they are thinking of and yet they are not influenced by it.

I know to whom Apulia has been allotted, who has Etruria, who the Picenian territory, who the Gallic district, who has begged for himself the office of spreading fire and sword by night through the city. They know that all the plans of the preceding night are brought to me. I laid them before the Senate yesterday. Catiline himself was alarmed, and fled. Why do these men wait? Verily, they are greatly mistaken if they think that former leniency of mine will last forever.

What I have been waiting for [is] that you should all see that a conspiracy has been openly formed against the Republic; unless, indeed, there be any one who thinks that those who are like Catiline do not agree with Catiline. There is not any longer room for leniency; the business itself demands severity. One thing, even now, I will grant: let them depart, let them be gone. Let them not suffer the unhappy Catiline to pine away for want of them. I will tell them the road. He went by the Aurelian road. If they make haste, they will catch him by the evening. O happy Republic, if it can cast forth these dregs of the Republic! Even now, when Catiline alone is got rid of; the Republic seems to me relieved and refreshed; for what evil or wickedness can be devised or imagined which he did not conceive? What prisoner, what gladiator, what thief; what assassin, what parricide, what forger of wills, what cheat, what debauchee, what spendthrift, what adulterer, what abandoned woman, what corrupter of youth, what profligate, what scoundrel can be found in all Italy, who does not avow that he has been on terms of intimacy with Catiline? What murder has been committed for years without him? What nefarious act of infamy that has not been done by him?

But in what other man were there ever so many allurements for youth as in him, who both indulged in infamous love for others, and encouraged their infamous affections for himself, promising to some enjoyment of their lust, to others the death of their parents, and not only instigating them to iniquity, but even assisting them in it. But now, how suddenly had he collected, not only out of the city, but even out of the country, a number of abandoned men? No one, not only at Rome, but in every corner of Italy, was overwhelmed with debt whom he did not enlist in this incredible association of wickedness.

And, that you may understand the diversity of his pursuits and the variety of his designs, there was no one in any school of gladiators, at all inclined to audacity, who does not avow himself to be an intimate friend of Catiline, no one on the stage, at all of a fickle and worthless disposition, who does not profess himself his companion. And he, trained in the practice of insult and wickedness, in enduring cold, and hunger, and thirst, and watching, was called a brave man by those fellows, while all the appliances of industry and instruments of virtue were devoted to lust and atrocity.

[His followers] think of nothing but slaughter, conflagration, and rapine. They have dissipated their patrimonies, they have squandered their fortunes. Money has long failed them, and now credit begins to fail; but the same desires remain which they had in their time of abundance: drinking and gambling parties ... embracing abandoned women, languid with wine, crammed with food ... reeking with ointments, worn out with lust....

But I am confident that some fate is hanging over these men; and that the punishment long since due to their iniquity, and worthlessness, and wickedness, and lust, is either visibly at hand or at least rapidly approaching. The only plots against us are within our own walls--the danger is within--the enemy is within. We must war with luxury, with madness, with wickedness. For this war, O citizens, I offer myself as the general. I take on myself the enmity of profligate men. What can be cured, I will cure, by whatever means it may be possible.

Yesterday, when I had been all but murdered at my own house, I convoked the Senate in the Temple of Jupiter Stator; I related the whole affair to the conscript fathers; and when Catiline came thither, what senator addressed him? Who saluted him? Who looked upon him not so much even as an abandoned citizen, as an implacable enemy? Nay, the chiefs of this body left that part of the benches to which he came, naked and empty. I suppose Manlius, that centurion who has pitched his camp in the Faesulan district, has proclaimed war against the Roman people in his own name; and that camp is not now waiting for Catiline as its general, and he, driven indeed into exile, will go to Marseilles, as they say, and not to that camp.

O the hard lot of those, not only of those who govern, but even of those who save the Republic. Now, if Lucius Catiline, hemmed in and rendered powerless by my counsels, by my toils, by my dangers, should on a sudden become alarmed, should change his designs, should desert his friends, should abandon his design of making war, should change his path from this course of wickedness and war, and betake himself to flight and exile, he will not be said to have been deprived by me of the arms of his audacity, to have been astounded and terrified by my diligence, to have been driven from his hope and from his enterprise, but, uncondemned and innocent, to have been driven into banishment by the Consul by threats and violence; and there will be some who will seek to have him thought not worthless but unfortunate, and be considered not a most active Consul, but a most cruel tyrant. I am not unwilling, O Romans, to endure this storm of false and unjust unpopularity as long as the danger of this horrible and nefarious war is warded off from you. Let him be said to be banished by me as long as he goes into banishment; but, believe me, he will not go. I will never ask of the immortal gods, O Romans, for the sake of lightening my own unpopularity, for you to hear that Lucius Catiline is leading an army of enemies, and is hovering about in arms; but yet in three days you will hear it. And I much more fear that it will be objected to me some day or other, that I have let him escape, rather than that I have banished him. But when there are men who say he has been banished because he has gone away, what would these men say if he had been put to death?

Although those men who keep saying that Catiline is going to Marseilles do not complain of this so much as they fear it; for there is not one of them so inclined to pity, as not to prefer that he should go to Manlius rather than to Marseilles. But he, if he had never before planned what he is now doing, yet would rather be slain while living as a bandit, than live as an exile; but now, when nothing has happened to him contrary to his own wish and design,—except, indeed, that he has left Rome while we are alive,—let us wish rather that he may go into exile than complain of it.

But why are we speaking so long about one enemy; and about that enemy who now avows that he is one; and whom I now do not fear, because, as I have always wished, a wall is between us; and are saying nothing about those who dissemble, who remain at Rome, who are among us? Whom, indeed, if it were by any means possible, I should be anxious not so much to chastise as to cure, and to make friendly to the Republic; nor, if they will listen to me, do I quite know why that may not be. For I will tell you, O Romans, of what classes of men those forces are made up, and then, if I can, I will apply to each the medicine of my advice and persuasion.

There is one class of them, who, with enormous debts, have still greater possessions, and who can by no means be detached from their affection to them. Of these men the appearance is most respectable, for they are wealthy, but their intention and their cause are most shameless. Will you be rich in lands, in houses, in money, in slaves, in all things, and yet hesitate to diminish your possessions to add to your credit? What are you expecting? War? What! in the devastation of all things, do you believe that your own possessions will be held sacred? do you expect an abolition of debts? They are mistaken who expect that from Catiline. There may be schedules made out, owing to my exertions, but they will be only catalogues of sale. Nor can those who have possessions be safe by any other means; and if they had been willing to adopt this plan earlier, and not, as is very foolish, to struggle on against usury with the profits of their farms, we should have them now richer and better citizens. But I think these men are the least of all to be dreaded, because they can either be persuaded to abandon their opinions, or if they cling to them, they seem to me more likely to form wishes against the Republic than to bear arms against it.

There is another class of them, who, although they are harassed by debt, yet are expecting supreme power; they wish to become masters. They think that when the Republic is in confusion they may gain those honors which they despair of when it is in tranquility. And they must, I think, be told the same as everyone else--to despair of obtaining what they are aiming at; that in the first place, I myself am watchful for, am present to, am providing for the Republic. Besides that, there is a high spirit in the virtuous citizens, great unanimity, great numbers, and also a great body of troops. Above all that, the immortal gods will stand by and bring aid to this invincible nation, this most illustrious empire, this most beautiful city, against such wicked violence. And if they had already got that which they with the greatest madness wish for, do they think that in the ashes of the city and blood of the citizens, which in their wicked and infamous hearts they desire, they will become Consuls and dictators and even kings? Do they not see that they are wishing for that which, if they were to obtain it, must be given up to some fugitive slave, or to some gladiator?

There is a third class, already touched by age, but still vigorous from constant exercise; of which class is Manlius himself; whom Catiline is now succeeding. These are men of those colonies which Sulla established at Faesulae, which I know to be composed, on the whole, of excellent citizens and brave men; but yet these are colonists, who, from becoming possessed of unexpected and sudden wealth, boast themselves extravagantly and insolently; these men, while they build like rich men, while they delight in farms, in litters, in vast families of slaves, in luxurious banquets, have incurred such great debts, that, if they would be saved, they must raise Sulla from the dead; and they have even excited some countrymen, poor and needy men, to entertain the same hopes of plunder as themselves. And all these men, O Romans, I place in the same class of robbers and banditti. But, I warn them, let them cease to be mad, and to think of proscriptions and dictatorships; for such a horror of these times is ingrained into the city, that not even men, but it seems to me that even the very cattle would refuse to bear them again.

There is a fourth class, various, promiscuous and turbulent; who indeed are now overwhelmed; who will never recover themselves; who, partly from indolence, partly from managing their affairs badly, partly from extravagance, are embarrassed by old debts; and worn out with bail bonds, and judgments, and seizures of their goods, are said to be betaking themselves in numbers to that camp both from the city and the country. These men I think not so much active soldiers as lazy insolvents; who, if they cannot stand at first, may fall, but fall so, that not only the city but even their nearest neighbors know nothing of it. For I do not understand why, if they cannot live with honor, they should wish to die shamefully; or wily they think they shall perish with less pain in a crowd, than if they perish by themselves.

There is a fifth class, of parricides, assassins, in short of all infamous characters, whom I do not wish to recall from Catiline, and indeed they cannot be separated from him. Let them perish in their wicked war, since they are so numerous that a prison cannot contain them.

There is a last class, last not only in number but in the sort of men and in their way of life; the especial bodyguard of Catiline, of his levying; yes, the friends of his embraces and of his bosom; whom you see with carefully combed hair, glossy, beardless, or with well-trimmed beards; with tunics with sleeves, or reaching to the ankles; clothed with veils, not with robes; all the industry of whose life, all the labor of whose watchfulness, is expended in suppers lasting till daybreak.

In these bands are all the gamblers, all the adulterers, all the unclean and shameless citizens. These boys, so witty and delicate, have learnt not only to love and to be loved, not only to sing and to dance, but also to brandish daggers and to administer poisons; and unless they are driven out, unless they die, even should Catiline die, I warn you that the school of Catiline would exist in the Republic. But what do those wretches want? Are they going to take their wives with them to the camp? how can they do without them, especially in these nights? and how will they endure the Apennines, and these frosts, and this snow? unless they think that they will bear the winter more easily because they have been in the habit of dancing naked at their feasts. O war much to be dreaded, when Catiline is going to have his bodyguard of prostitutes!

Array now, O Romans, against these splendid troops of Catiline, your guards and your armies; and first of all oppose to that worn-out and wounded gladiator your Consuls and generals; then against that banished and enfeebled troop of ruined men lead out the flower and strength of all Italy instantly the cities of the colonies and municipalities will match the rustic mounds of Catiline; and I will not condescend to compare the rest of your troops and equipment and guards with the want and destitution of that highwayman. But if, omitting all these things in which we are rich and of which he is destitute,—the Senate, the Roman knights, the people, the city, the treasury, the revenues, all Italy, all the provinces, foreign nations,—if I say, omitting all these things, we choose to compare the causes themselves which are opposed to one another, we may understand from that alone how thoroughly prostrate they are. For on the one side are fighting modesty, on the other wantonness; on the one chastity, on the other uncleanness; on the one honesty, on the other fraud; on the one piety, on the other wickedness; on the one consistency, on the other insanity; on the one honor, on the other baseness; on the one continence, on the other lust; in short, equity, temperance, fortitude, prudence, all the virtues contend against iniquity with luxury, against indolence, against rashness, against all the vices; lastly, abundance contends against destitution, good plans against baffled designs, wisdom against madness, well-founded hope against universal despair. In a contest and war of this sort, even if the zeal of men were to fail, will not the immortal gods compel such numerous and excessive vices to be defeated by these most eminent virtues?

And as this is the case, O Romans, as I have said before, defend your house with guards and vigilance. I have taken care and made arrangements that there shall be sufficient protection for the city without distressing you and without any tumult. All the colonists and citizens of your municipal towns, being informed by me of this nocturnal sally of Catiline, will easily defend their cities and territories; the gladiators which he thought would be his most numerous and most trusty band, although they are better disposed than part of the patricians, will be held in cheek by our power. Quintus Metellus, whom I, making provision for this, sent on to the Gallic and Picenian territory, will either overwhelm the man, or will prevent all his motions and attempts; but with respect to the arrangement of all other matters, and maturing and acting on our plans, we shall consult the Senate, which, as you are aware, is convened.

Now once more I wish those who have remained in the city, and who, contrary to the safety of the city and of all of you, have been left in the city by Catiline, although they are enemies, yet because they were born citizens, to be warned again and again by me. If my leniency has appeared to any one too remiss, it has been only waiting that that might break out which was lying hid. As to the future, I cannot now forget that this is my country, that I am the Consul of these citizens; that I must either live with them, or die for them. There is no guard at the gate, no one plotting against their path; if any one wishes to go, he can provide for himself; but if any one stirs in the city, and if I detect not only any action, but any attempt or design against the country, he shall feel that there are in this city vigilant Consuls, eminent magistrates, a brave Senate, arms, and prisons; which our ancestors appointed as the avengers of nefarious and convicted crimes.

And all this shall be so done, O Romans, that affairs of the greatest importance shall be transacted with the least possible disturbance; the greatest dangers shall be avoided without any tumult; an internal civil war the most cruel and terrible in the memory of man, shall be put an end to by me alone in the robe of peace acting as general and commander-in-chief. And this I will so arrange, O Romans, that if it can be by any means managed, even the most worthless man shall not suffer the punishment of his crimes in this city. But if the violence of open audacity, if danger impending over the Republic drives me of necessity from this merciful disposition, at all events I will manage this, which seems scarcely even to be hoped for in so great and so treacherous a war, that no good man shall fall, and that you may all be saved by the punishment of a few.

And I promise you this, O Romans, relying neither on my own prudence, nor on human counsels, but on many and manifest intimations of the will of the immortal gods; under whose guidance I first entertained this hope and this opinion; who are now defending their temples and the houses of the city, not far off, as they were used to, from a foreign and distant enemy, but here on the spot, by their own divinity and present help. And you, O Romans, ought to pray to and implore them to defend from the nefarious wickedness of abandoned citizens, now that all the forces of all enemies are defeated by land and sea, this city which they have ordained to be the most beautiful and flourishing of all cities.

CICERO'S THIRD ORATION AGAINST CATILINE

Translated by C.D. Yonge, abridged

[On this day,] O Romans, the Republic, and all your lives, your goods, your fortunes, your wives and children, this home of most illustrious empire, thus most fortunate and beautiful city, by the great love of the immortal gods for you, by my labors and counsels and dangers, snatched from fire and sword, and almost from the very jaws of fate, and preserved and restored to you.

When I found that the ambassadors of the Allobroges had been tampered with by Publius Lentulus, for the sake of exciting a Transalpine war and commotion in Gaul, and that they, on their return to Gaul, had been sent with letters and messages to Catiline on the same road, and that Vulturcius had been added to them as a companion, and that he too had had letters given him for Catiline, I thought that an opportunity was given me of contriving ... that the whole business might be manifestly detected not by me alone, but by the Senate also, and by you.

Therefore, yesterday I summoned Lucius Flaccus and C. Pomtinus, the praetors, brave men and well-affected to the Republic. I explained to them the whole matter, and showed them what I wished to have done. They, full of noble and worthy sentiments towards the Republic, without hesitation, and without any delay, undertook the business, and when it was evening, went secretly to the Mulvian Bridge, and there so distributed themselves in the nearest villas, that the Tiber and the bridge was between them. And they took to the same place, without any one having the least suspicion of it, many brave men, and I had sent many picked young men of the prefecture of Reate, whose assistance I constantly employ in the protection of the Republic, armed with swords. In the meantime, about the end of the third watch, when the ambassadors of the Allobroges, with a great retinue and Vulturcius with them, began to come upon the Mulvian Bridge, an attack is made upon them; swords are drawn both by them and by our people; the matter was understood by the praetors alone, but was unknown to the rest.

Then, by the intervention of Pomtinus and Flaccus, the fight which had begun was put an end to; all the letters which were in the hands of the whole company are delivered to the praetors with time seals unbroken; the men themselves are arrested and brought to me at daybreak. I quickly summoned a full Senate, as you saw; and meantime, without any delay, by the advice of the Allobroges, I sent Caius Sulpicius the praetor, a brave man, to bring whatever arms he could find in the house of Cethegus, whence he did bring a great number of swords and daggers.

I introduced Vulturcius without the Gauls. By the command of the Senate, I pledged him the public faith for his safety. I exhorted him fearlessly to tell all he knew. Then, when he had scarcely recovered himself from his great alarm, he said: that he had messages and letters for Catiline, from Publius Lentulus, to avail himself of the guard of the slaves, and to come towards the city with his army as quickly as possible; and that was to be done with the intention that, when they had set fire to the city on all sides as it had been arranged and distributed, and had made a great massacre of the citizens, he might be at hand to catch those who fled, and to join himself to the leaders within the city. But the Gauls being introduced, said that an oath had been administered to them, and letters given them by Publius Lentulus, Cethegus, and Statilius, for their nation; and that they had been enjoined by them, and by Lucius Cassius, to send cavalry into Italy as early as possible; that infantry should not be wanting; and that Lentulus had assured him, from the Sibylline oracles and the answers of soothsayers, that he was that third Cornelius to whom the kingdom and sovereignty over this city was fated to come; that Cinna and Sulla had been before him; and that he had also said that was the year destined to the destruction of this city and empire, being the tenth year after the acquittal of the Virgins, and the twentieth after the burning of the Capitol. But they said there had been this dispute between Cethegus and the rest--that Lentulus and others thought it best that the massacre should take place and the city be burnt at the Saturnalia, but that Cethegus thought it too long to wait.

And, not to detain you, O Romans, we ordered the letters to be brought forward which were said to have been given them by each of the men. First I showed his seal to Cethegus; he recognized it: we cut the thread; we read the letter. It was written with his own hand: that he would do for the Senate and people of the Allobroges what he had promised their ambassadors; and that he begged them also to do what their ambassadors had arranged. Then Cethegus, who a little before had made answer about the swords and daggers which had been found in his house, and had said that he had always been fond of fine arms, being stricken down and dejected at the reading of his letters, convicted by his own conscience, became suddenly silent. Statilius, being introduced, owned his handwriting and his seal. His letters were read, of nearly the same tenor: he confessed it. Then I showed Lentulus his letters, and asked him whether he recognized the seal? He nodded assent. Then Gabinius being introduced, when at first he had begun to answer impudently, at last denied nothing of those things which the Gauls alleged against him. And to me, indeed, O Romans, though the letters, the seals, the handwriting, and the confession of each individual seemed most certain indications and proofs of wickedness, yet their color, their eyes, their countenance, their silence, appeared more certain still; for they stood so stupefied, they kept their eyes so fixed on the ground, at times looking stealthily at one another, that they appeared now not so much to be informed against by others as to be informing against themselves.

Having produced and divulged these proofs, O Romans, I consulted the Senate what ought to be done for the interests of the Republic. Vigorous and fearless opinions were delivered by the chief men, which the Senate adopted without any variety; and since the decree of the Senate is not yet written out, I will relate to you from memory, O citizens, what the Senate has decreed. First of all, a vote of thanks to me is passed in the most honorable words, because the Republic has been delivered from the greatest dangers by my valor and wisdom, and prudence. They voted that Publius Lentulus, when he had abdicated the praetorship, should be given into custody; and also, that Caius Cethegus, Lucius Statilius, Publius Gabinius, who were all present, should be given into custody: and the same decree was passed against Lucius Cassius, who had begged for himself the office of burning the city; against Marcus Caparius, to whom it had been proved that Apulia had been allotted for the purpose of exciting disaffection among the shepherds; against Publius Furius, who belongs to the colonies which Lucius Sulla led to Faesulae; against Quintus Manlius Chilo, who was always associated with this man Furius in his tampering with the Allobroges; against Publius Umbrenus, a freedman, by whom it was proved that the Gauls were originally brought to Gabinius.

Now, since, O citizens you have the nefarious leaders of this most wicked and dangerous war taken prisoners and in your grasp, you ought to think that all the resources of Catiline--all his hopes and all his power, now that these dangers of the city are warded off, have fallen to pieces. And, indeed, when I drove him from the city I foresaw in my mind, O citizens, that if Catiline were removed, I had no cause to fear either the drowsiness of Publius Lentulus, or the fat of Lucius Cassius, or the mad rashness of Cassius Cethegus. He alone was to be feared of all these men, and that, only as long as he was within the walls of the city. He knew everything, he had access to everybody. He had the skill and the audacity to address, to tempt and to tamper with everyone. He had acuteness suited to crime; and neither tongue nor hand ever failed to support that acuteness. Already he had men he could rely on chosen and distributed for the execution of all other business and when he had ordered anything to be done he did not think it was done on that account. There was nothing to which he did not personally attend and see to--for which he did not watch and toil. He was able to endure cold, thirst, and hunger.

Who, O Romans can there be so obstinate against the truth, so headstrong, so void of sense, as to deny that all these things which we see, and especially this city, is governed by the divine authority and power of the immortal gods? He, Jupiter, resisted [the conspirators]. He determined that the Capitol should be safe, he saved these temples, he saved this city, he saved all of you. It is under the guidance of the immortal gods, O Romans, that I have cherished the intention and desires which I have, and have arrived at such undeniable proofs. Surely, that tampering with the Allobroges would never have taken place, so important a matter would never have been so madly entrusted, by Lentulus and the rest of our internal enemies, to strangers and foreigners, such letters would never have been written, unless all prudence had been taken by the immortal gods from such terrible audacity. What shall I say? That Gauls, men from a state scarcely at peace with us, the only nation existing which seems both to be able to make war on the Roman people, and not to be unwilling to do so that they should disregard the hope of empire and of the greatest success voluntarily offered to them by patricians; and should prefer your safety to their own power--do you not think that that was caused by divine interposition? especially when they could have destroyed us, not by fighting, but by keeping silence.

Since it is now night, O Romans, worship Jupiter, the guardian of this city and of yourselves, and depart to your homes; and defend those homes, though the danger is now removed, with guard and watch as you did last night, that you shall not have to do so long, and that you shall enjoy perpetual tranquility, shall, O Romans, be my care.

CICERO'S FOURTH ORATION AGAINST CATILINE

Translated by C.D. Yonge, abridged

I see that the looks and eyes of you all are turned towards me; I see that you are anxious not only for your own danger and that of the Republic, but even, if that be removed, for mine. Your good-will is delightful to one amid evils, and pleasing amid grief; but I entreat you, in the name of the immortal gods, lay it aside now, and, forgetting my safety, think of yourselves and of your children. If indeed, this condition of the consulship has been allotted to me, that I should bear all bitterness, all pains and tortures, I will bear them not only bravely but even cheerfully, provided that by my toils dignity and safety are procured for you and for the Roman people.

I am that Consul to whom neither the forum in which all justice is contained, nor the Campus Martius, consecrated to the consular assemblies, nor the Senate house, the chief assistance of all nations, nor my own home, the common refuge of all men, nor my bed devoted to rest, in short, not even this seat of honor, this curule chair has ever been free from the danger of death, or from plots and treachery. I have been silent about many things, I have borne much, I have conceded much, I have remedied many things with some pain to myself amid the alarm of you all. Now if the immortal gods have determined that there shall be this end to my consulship that I should snatch you and the Roman people from miserable slaughter, your wives and children and the Vestal Virgins from most bitter distress, the temples and shrines of the gods and this most lovely country of all of us, from impious flames, all Italy from war and devastation, then whatever fortune is laid up for me by myself it shall be borne. If, indeed, Publius Lentulus, being led on by soothsayers believed that his name was connected by destiny with the destruction of the Republic, why should not I rejoice that my consulship has taken place almost by the express appointment of fate for the preservation of the Republic?

[The conspirators] are now in your hands who withstood all Rome, with the object of bringing conflagration on the whole city, massacre on all of you, and of receiving Catiline; their letters are in your possession, their seals, their handwriting, and the confession of each individual of them; the Allobroges are tampered with, the slaves are excited, Catiline is sent for; the design is actually begun to be put in execution, that all should be put to death, so that no one should be left even to mourn the name of the Republic, and to lament over the downfall of so mighty a dominion.

All these things the witnesses have informed you of; the prisoners have confessed, you by many judgments have already decided; first, because you have thanked me in unprecedented language, and have passed a vote that the conspiracy of abandoned men has been laid open by my virtue and diligence; secondly, because you have compelled Publius Lentulus to abdicate the praetorship; again, because you have voted that he and the others about whom you have decided should be given into custody; and above all because you have decreed a supplication in my name, an honor which has never been paid to any one before acting in a civil capacity; last of all because yesterday you gave most ample rewards to the ambassadors of the Allobroges and to Titus Vulturcius; all which acts are such that they, who have been given into custody by name, without any doubt seem already condemned by you.

But I have determined to refer the business to you as a fresh matter, both as to the fact, what you think of it and as to the punishment, what you vote. I will state what it behooves the Consul to state. I have seen for a long time great madness existing in the Republic, and new designs being formed, and evil passions being stirred up; but I never thought that so great, so destructive a conspiracy as this was being meditated by citizens. Now to whatever point your minds and opinions incline, you must decide before night. You see how great a crime has been made known to you; if you think that but few are implicated in it you are greatly mistaken; this evil has spread wider than you think; it has spread not only throughout Italy, but it has even crossed the Alps, and creeping stealthily on, it has already occupied many of the provinces; it can by no means be crushed by tolerating it, and by temporizing with it; however you determine on chastising it, you must act with promptitude.

I see that as yet there are two opinions. One that of Decius Silanus, who thinks that those who have endeavored to destroy all these things should be punished with death, the other, that of Caius Caesar, who objects to the punishment of death, but adopts the most extreme severity of all other punishment. Each acts in a manner suitable to his own dignity and to the magnitude of the business with the greatest severity. The one thinks that it is not right that those, who have attempted to deprive all of us and the while Roman people of life, to destroy the empire, to extinguish the name of the Roman people, should enjoy life and the breath of heaven common to us all, for one moment; and he remembers that this sort of punishment has often been employed against worthless citizens in this Republic. The other feels that death was not appointed by the immortal gods for the sake of punishment, but that it is either a necessity of nature, or a rest from toils and miseries; therefore wise men have never met it unwillingly, brave men have often encountered it even voluntarily. But imprisonment and that too perpetual, was certainly invented for the extraordinary punishment of nefarious wickedness; therefore he proposes that they should be distributed among the municipal towns. This proposition seems to have in it injustice if you command; it difficulty if you request it.

[Had we not acted in time, I see] this city, the light of the world and the citadel of all nations, falling on a sudden by one conflagration. I see in my mind's eye miserable and unburied heaps of cities in my buried country; the sight of Cethegus and his madness raging amid your slaughter is ever present to my sight. But when I have set before myself Lentulus reigning, as he himself confesses that he had hoped was his destiny, and this Gabinius arrayed in the purple and Catiline arrived with his army, then I shudder at the lamentation of matrons, and the flight of Virgins and of boys and the insults of the Vestal Virgins; and because these things appear to me exceedingly miserable and pitiable, therefore I show myself severe and rigorous to those who have wished to bring about this state of things. I ask, forsooth, if any father of a family, supposing his children had been slain by a slave, his wife murdered, his house burnted, were not to inflict on his slaves the severest possible punishment would he appear clement and merciful or most inhuman and cruel? To me he would seem unnatural and hard-hearted who did not soothe his own pain and anguish by the pain and torture of the criminal. And so we, in the case of these men who desired to murder us, and our wives, and our children, who endeavored to destroy the houses of every individual among us, and also the Republic, the home of all, who designed to place the nation of the Allobroges on the relics of this city, and on the ashes of the empire destroyed by fire; if we are very rigorous, we shall be considered merciful; if we choose to be lax, we must endure the character of the greatest cruelty, to the damage of our country and our fellow-citizens.

[Even now, Cicero warns senators, a slave] of Lentulus is running about the shops,—is hoping that the minds of some poor and ignorant men may be corrupted by bribery; that, indeed, has been attempted and begun, but no one has been found either so wretched in their fortune or so abandoned in their inclination as not to wish the place of their seat and work and daily gain, their chamber and their bed, and, in short, the tranquil course of their lives, to be still preserved to them. And far the greater part of those who are in the shops, the whole of this class is of all the most attached to tranquility; their whole stock, indeed, their whole employment and livelihood, exists by the peaceful intercourse of the citizens, and is wholly supported by peace. And if their gains are diminished whenever their shops are shut, what will they be when they are burned? And, as this is the case, the protection of the Roman people is not wanting to you; do you take care that you do not seem to be wanting to the Roman people.

You have a Consul preserved out of many dangers and plots, and from death itself not for his own life, but for your safety. All ranks agree for the preservation of the Republic with heart and will, with zeal, with virtue, with their voice. Your common country, besieged by the hands and weapons of an impious conspiracy, stretches forth her hands to you as a suppliant; to you she recommends herself to you she recommends the lives of all the citizens, and the citadel, and the Capitol, and the altars of the household gods, and the eternal inextinguishable fire of Vesta, and all the temples of all the gods, and the altars and the walls and the houses of the city. Moreover, your own lives, those of your wives and children, the fortunes of all men, your homes, your hearth; are this day interested in your decision.

You have a leader mindful of you, forgetful of himself, an opportunity which is not always given to men; you have all ranks, all individuals, the whole Roman people [a thing which in civil transactions we see this day for the first time], full of one and the same feeling. As numerous as is the band of conspirators--and you see that it is very great--so numerous a multitude of enemies do I see that I have brought upon myself. But I consider them base and powerless and despicable and abject. But even if at any time that band shall be excited by the wickedness and madness of anyone, and shall show itself more powerful than your dignity and that of the Republic, I shall never repent of my actions and of my advice. Death, indeed, which they perhaps threaten me with, is prepared for all men; such glory during life as you have honored me with by your decrees no one has ever attained to. For you have passed votes of congratulation to others for having governed the Republic successfully, but to me alone for having saved it

Let Scipio be thought illustrious, he by whose wisdom and velour Hannibal was compelled to return into Africa, and to depart from Italy. Let the second Africanus be extolled with conspicuous praise, who destroyed two cities most hostile to this empire, Carthage and Numantia. Let Lucius Paullus be thought a great man, he whose triumphal car was graced by Perses, previously a most powerful and noble monarch. Let Marius be held in eternal honor, who twice delivered Italy from siege, and from the fear of slavery. Let Pompey be preferred to them all—Pompey, whose exploits and whose virtues are bounded by the same districts and limits as the course of the sun. There will be, among the praises of these men, some room for my glory. I see that an eternal war with all wicked citizens has been undertaken by me; which, however, I am confident can easily be driven back from me and mine by your aid, and by that of all good men.

Wherefore, determine with care, as you have begun, and boldly, concerning your own safety, and that of the Roman people, and concerning your wives and children; concerning your altars and your hearths your shrines and temples; concerning the houses and homes of the whole city; concerning your dominion, your liberty and the safety of Italy and the whole Republic. For you have a Consul who will not hesitate to obey your decrees, and who will be able as long as he lives, to defend what you decide on and of his own power to execute it.

APPENDIX B

CAESAR'S ORATION AGAINST THE DEATH PENALTY FOR THE CONSPIRATORS

It becomes all men who deliberate on dubious matters, to be influenced neither by hatred, affection, anger, nor pity. When the mind is freely exerted, its reasoning is sound: but passion, if it gain possession of it, becomes its tyrant, and reason is powerless.

I could easily mention, conscript fathers, numerous examples of kings and nations, who, swayed by resentment or compassion, have adopted injudicious courses of conduct; but I had rather speak of those instances in which our ancestors, in opposition to the impulse of passion, acted with wisdom and sound policy.

In the Macedonian War, which we carried on against king Perses, the great and powerful state of Rhodes, which had risen by the aid of the Roman people, was faithless and hostile to us: yet, when the war was ended, and the conduct of the Rhodians was taken into consideration, our forefathers left them unmolested, lest any should say that war was made upon them for the sake of seizing their wealth, rather than of punishing their faithlessness. Throughout the Punic Wars, too, the Carthaginians, both during peace and in suspensions of arms, were guilty of many acts of injustice, yet our ancestors never took occasion to retaliate, but considered rather what was worthy of themselves, than what might justly be inflicted on their enemies. [In reality, as we saw earlier in the book, Carthaginians were massacred, the survivors sold into slavery, the land salted.]

Similar caution is to be observed by yourselves, that the guilt of Lentulus, and the other conspirators, may not have greater weight with you than your own dignity, and that you may not regard your indignation more than your character. If, indeed, a punishment adequate to their crimes be discovered, I consent to extraordinary measures; but if the enormity of their crime exceeds whatever can be devised, I think that we should inflict only such penalties as the laws have provided.

Most of those, who have given their opinions before me, have deplored, in studied and impressive language, the sad fate that threatens the republic; they have recounted the barbarities of war, and the afflictions that would fall on the vanquished; they have told us that maidens would be dishonored, and youths abused; that children would be torn from the embraces of their parents; that matrons would be subjected to the pleasure of the conquerors; that temples and dwelling-houses would be plundered; that massacres and fires would follow; and that every place would be filled with arms, corpses, blood, and lamentation. But to what end, in the name of the eternal gods! was such eloquence directed? Was it intended to render you indignant at the conspiracy? A speech, no doubt, will inflame him whom so frightful and monstrous a reality has not provoked! Far from it: for to no man does evil, directed against himself, appear a light matter; many, on the contrary, have felt it more seriously than was right.

But to different persons different degrees of license are allowed. If those who pass a life sunk in obscurity, commit any error, through excessive anger, few become aware of it, for their fame is as limited as their fortune; but of those who live invested with extensive power, and in an exalted station, the whole world knows the proceedings. Thus in the highest position there is the least liberty of action; and it becomes us to indulge neither partiality nor aversion, but least of all animosity; for what in others is called resentment, is in the powerful termed violence and cruelty.

I am indeed of opinion that the utmost degree of torture is inadequate to punish their crime; but the generality of mankind dwell on that which happens last, and, in the case of malefactors, forget their guilt, and talk only of their punishment, should that punishment have been inordinately severe. I feel assured, too, that Decimus Silanus, a man of spirit and resolution, made the suggestions which he offered, from zeal for the State, and that he had no view, in so important a matter, to favor or to enmity; such I know to be his character, and such his discretion. Yet his proposal appears to me, I will not say cruel [for what can be cruel that is directed against such characters?], but foreign to our policy. For assuredly, Silanus, either your fears, or their treason, must have induced you, a Consul-elect, to propose this new kind of punishment. Of fear it is unnecessary to speak, when, by the prompt activity of that distinguished man our Consul, such numerous forces are under arms; and as to the punishment we may say, what is indeed the truth, that in trouble and distress, death is a relief from suffering, and not a torment; that it puts an end to all human woes; and that, beyond it, there is no place either for sorrow or joy.

But why, in the name of the immortal gods, did you not add to your proposal, Silanus, that, before they were put to death, they should be punished with the scourge? Was it because the Porcian Law forbids it? But other laws forbid condemned citizens to be deprived of life, and allow them to go into exile. Or was it because scourging is a severer penalty than death? Yet what can be too severe, or too harsh, toward men convicted of such an offense? But if scourging be a milder punishment than death, how is it consistent to observe the law as to the smaller point, when you disregard it as to the greater?

But who, it may be asked, will blame any severity that shall be decreed against these parricides of their country? I answer that time, the course of events, and fortune, whose caprice governs nations, may blame it. Whatever shall fall on the traitors, will fall on them justly; but it is for you to consider well what you resolve to inflict on others. All precedents productive of evil effects have had their origin from what was good; but when a government passes into the hands of the ignorant or unprincipled, any new example of severity, inflicted on deserving and suitable objects, is extended to those that are improper and undeserving of it. The Spartans, when they had conquered the Athenians, appointed thirty men to govern their state. These thirty began their administration by putting to death, even without a trial, all who were notoriously wicked, or publicly detestable--acts at which the people rejoiced, and extolled their justice. But afterward, when their lawless power gradually increased, they proceeded, at their pleasure, to kill the good and bad indiscriminately, and to strike terror into all; and thus the State, overpowered and enslaved, paid a heavy penalty for its imprudent exultation.

Within our own memory, too, when the victorious Sulla ordered Damasippus, and others of similar character, who had risen by distressing their country, to be put to death, who did not commend the proceeding? All exclaimed that wicked and factious men, who had troubled the State with their seditious practices, had justly forfeited their lives. Yet this proceeding was the commencement of great bloodshed. For whenever anyone coveted the mansion or villa, or even the plate or apparel of another, he exerted his influence to have him numbered among the proscribed. Thus they, to whom the death of Damasippus had been a subject of joy, were soon after dragged to death themselves; nor was there any cessation of slaughter, until Sulla had glutted all his partisans with riches.

Such excesses, indeed, I do not fear from Marcus Tullius, or in these times. But in a large state there arise many men of various dispositions. At some other period, and under another Consul, who, like the present, may have an army at his command, some false accusation may be credited as true; and when, with our example for a precedent, the Consul shall have drawn the sword on the authority of the Senate, who shall stay its progress, or moderate its fury?

Our ancestors were never deficient in conduct or courage; nor did pride prevent them from imitating the customs of other nations, if they appeared deserving of regard. Their armor, and weapons of war, they borrowed from the Samnites; their ensigns of authority, for the most part, from the Etrurians; and, in short, whatever appeared eligible to them, whether among allies or among enemies, they adopted at home with the greatest readiness, being more inclined to emulate merit than to be jealous of it. But at the same time, adopting a practice from Greece, they punished their citizens with the scourge, and inflicted capital punishment on such as were condemned. When the Republic, however, became powerful, and faction grew strong from the vast number of citizens, men began to involve the innocent in condemnation, and other like abuses were practiced; and it was then that the Porcian and other laws were provided, by which condemned citizens were allowed to go into exile. This lenity of our ancestors I regard as a very strong reason why we should not adopt any new measures of severity. For assuredly there was greater merit and wisdom in those who raised so mighty an empire from humble means, than in us, who can scarcely preserve what they so honorably acquired. Am I of opinion, then, you will ask, that the conspirators should be set free, and that the army of Catiline should thus be increased? Far from it: my recommendation is, that their property be confiscated, and that they themselves be kept in custody in such of the municipal towns as are best able to bear the expense; that noon hereafter bring their case to the Senate, or speak on it to the people, and that the Senate now give their opinion that he who shall act contrary to this will act against the Republic and the general safety.

Cicero.

As a noble he felt that the plebes were men not only swayed by passion and not reason, but dangerous. As a ''new man'' he desired to become part of the reigning aristocracy, the Optimates, and because he was frail and physically week, they thought they could control him, up to the time he took ascendancy over them all. He was no Cato, and although he did defend certain moral causes--and didn't hesitate to make mortal enemies of Caesar and Mark Antony--he at times folded to certain pressures, detailed elsewhere in this book. His speeches, wonders, were often amusing, especially when he reminded the people how lucky they were to have him. But in general he was intransigent and blindly reactionary, yet he was a veritable Republican right up to the moment his head was struck from his body.

APPENDIX C

THE LEX VALERIA

The seizure of power by Sulla, his sending troops into the Forum, inspired the conspiracies of Catiline, followed by Caesar's crossing of the Rubicon and *his* entry into Rome.

Sulla was responsible for the killing of thousands of Roman citizens, through a Civil War and proscriptions. The Lex Valeria of 82 B.C. gave Sulla dictatorial *imperium*, the first man so empowered since the Punic

Wars, 100 years earlier.

Caesar became dictator when he followed Sulla's example, his dictatorship taken up by those who followed, under the name of emperor.

These were Sulla's powers under the Lex Valeria:

1] He had the power to execute anyone without trial.

2] He could initiate legislation.

3] There was no time limit to his nomination [which had been, until then, for a period of six months].

4] He could decide the criteria for becoming a senator: who was admissible, their age and the number of senators, that he increased from 300 to 600.

5] He was allowed to end the grain distributions put into effect by Gaius Gracchus, thus ending subsidies.

After his death the above was overturned.

SOURCES

The major sources consulted or used in the writing of this book:

Aelianus was a Roman author and teacher of rhetoric who spoke and wrote in Greek.

Aeschylus, of whom 7 out of perhaps 90 plays have survived. His gravestone celebrated his heroism during the victory against the Persians at Marathon and *not his plays*, proof of the extraordinary importance of Greek survival against the barbarians(sadly, he lost his brother at Marathon). He is said to have been a deeply religious person, dedicated to Zeus. As a boy he worked in a vineyard until Dionysus visited him in a dream and directed him to write plays. One of his plays supposedly divulged too much about the Eleusinian Mysteries and he was nearly stoned to death by the audience. He had to stand trial but pleaded ignorance. He got off when the judges learned of the death of his brother at Marathon and when Aeschylus showed the wounds he and a second brother had received at Marathon too, the second brother left with but a stump in place of his hand. In one of his later plays Pericles was part of the chorus. The subjects of his plays often concerned Troy and the Persian Wars, Marathon, Salamis and Xerxes (Xerxes is accused of losing the war due to hubris; his building of the bridge over the Hellespont was a show of arrogance the gods found unacceptable). In *Seven against Thebes* he relates the destinies of Oedipus' two sons who agree to become kings of Thebes on alternate years. Naturally, when the time comes for them to change places the king in place refuses, which leads to both boys killing each other. *Agamemnon* is an excellent retelling of the Trojan War, as Agamemnon sails home to be murdered by his wife Clytemnestra. In *The Libation Bearers* Agamemnon's boy Orestes returns home to destroy his father's assassins, Clytemnestra and her lover Aegisthus. In *The Eumenides* (the Kindly Spirits) Orestes is chased by the Furies for having killed his mother. He takes shelter with Apollo who decides, with Athena, to try the boy before a court. The vote is a tie, but Athena, preaching the importance of reason and understanding, acquits him. She then changes the terrible Furies into sweet Eumenides.

Anacreon was born in 582 B.C. and was known for his drinking songs.

Andocides was implicated in the Hermes scandal and saved his skin by turning against Alcibiades in a speech that has come down to us called, what else?, *Against Alcibiades*.

Appian, who lived during the reigns of Trajan and Hadrian, was a Roman historian of Greek origin. He was a friend of Fronto, Marcus Aurelius' tutor and, perhaps, lover. He left his book, *Roman History*, which describes, among other events, the Roman civil wars.

Aristophanes, my preferred playwright, is, naturally, the father of comedy. He wrote perhaps 40 plays of which 11 remain. He was feared by all: Plato states that it was his play *The Clouds* the root of the trial that cost Socrates his life. Nearly nothing is known about him other than what he himself revealed in his works. Playwrights were obliged to be conservative because part of each play was funded by a wealthy citizen, an honor for the citizen and a caveat for the author. He was an exponent of make-love-not-war who saw his country go from its wonderful defeat of the Persians to its end at the hands of the Spartans. Along with Alcibiades and Socrates, Aristophanes is featured in Plato's *The Symposium* in which he is gently mocked, proof that he was considered, even by those he poked fun at, as affable. *The Acharnians* highlights the troubles the Athenians went through after the death of Pericles and their defeat at the hands of Sparta. *The Peace* focuses on the Peace of Nicias. *Lysistrata* tells about the plight of women trying to bring about peace in order to prevent the sacrifice of their sons during war, occasioning the world's first sex strike. When Athens lost its freedom to Sparta, Aristophanes stopped writing plays.

Athenaeus lived in the times of Marcus Aurelius. His *Deipnosopistae* is a banquet conversation *à la Platon* during which conversations on every possible subject takes place, filling fifteen books that have come down to us.

Ausonius was a Latin poet and teacher of rhetoric, around 350 B.C.

Bion was a Greek philosopher known for his diatribes, satires and attacks on religion. He lived around 300 B.C.

Cassius Dio, 155 A.D. to 235 A.D., was a noted historian who wrote in Greek and published a history of Rome in 80 volumes, many of which have survived, giving modern historians a detailed look into his times.

Cicero was born in 106 B.C. and murdered by Mark Antony in 43 B.C. Michael Grant said it all when he wrote, ''the influence of Cicero upon the history of European literature and ideas greatly exceeds that of any other prose writer in any language.''

Cornelius Nepos was a Roman friend of Cicero. Most of what he wrote was lost, so what we know comes through passages of his works in the books of other historians.

Ctesias was a Greek historian from Anatolian Caria, and the physican of Artaxerxes, whom he accompanied in his war against his brother Cyrus the Younger. He wrote a book on India, *Indica* and Persia, *Persica*. The fragments we have of his writing come to us through Diodorus Siculus and Plutarch.

Diodorus Siculus lived around 50 B.C. and wrote *Historical Library*, consisting of forty volumes.

Diogenes of Sinope (aka Diogenes the Cynic) comes to use through extracts of his writing passed on by others, as nothing he wrote has survived. He had a truly remarkable life, at first imprisoned for debasing the coins his father, a banker, minted. Afterwards he pled poverty, sleeping in a huge ceramic jar, walking the streets of Athens during the day with a lighted lamp, saying he was in search of an honest man, and teasing Plato by noisily eating through his lectures (later Plato claimed he was ''a Socrates gone mad''.) On a voyage he was captured and sold as a slave in Crete to a Corinthian who was so entranced by his intelligence that he made him his sons' teacher. It was in his master's household that he grew old and died. Plutarch tells us he met Alexander the Great while Diogenes was staring at a pile of bones. In answer to Alexander's question he said he was searching for the bones of Alexander's father, but could not distinguish them from those of a slave. Alexander supposedly said that if he couldn't be Alexander he would choose to be Diogenes. He was the first man ever to claim to be ''a citizen of the world.'' He urinated on people, defecated where he would and masturbated in public, about which he said, ''If only I could banish hunger by rubbing my belly.'' The word cynic meant dog-like, and when someone questioned him about it he said he too was dog-like because he licked those who helped him, barked at those who didn't, and bit his enemies. Rogers and Hart wrote these lyrics about him: There was an old zany/who lived in a tub; he had so many flea-bites/he didn't know where to rub.

Eupolis lived around 430 B.C. An Athenian poet who wrote during the Peloponnesian Wars.

Euripides may have written 90 plays of which 18 survive. His approach was a study of the inner lives of his personages, the predecessor of Shakespeare. Due to his stance on certain subjects, he thought it best to leave Athens voluntarily rather than suffer an end similar to that of Socrates. An example: ''I would prefer to stand three times to confront my enemies in battle rather than bear a single child!'' He was born on the island of Salamis, of Persian-War fame; in fact he was born on the very day of the battle. His youth was spent in athletics and dance. Due to bad marriages with unfaithful wives, he withdrew to Salamis where he wrote while contemplating sea and sky. When Sparta defeated Athens in war, it did not burn the city to the ground: Plutarch states that this was thanks to one of Euripides' plays, *Electra*, put on for the Spartans in Athens, a play they found so wonderful that they proclaimed that it would be barbarous to destroy a city capable of engendering men of the quality of Euripides. (The real reason was to preserve the city that had twice saved Greece from Persian victory.) Euripides was known for his love of Agathon, a youth praised for his beauty as well as for his culture, and would later become a playwright. Aristophanes mocked Euripides for loving Agathon long after he had left his boyhood behind him. (Remember, not everyone followed boy-love to the letter. The idea of men loving boys until they grew whiskers did not always hold true. Boys grown ''old'' could shave their chins and butts; some men just preferred other men, hairy or not, while most men impregnated boys but other men adored being penetrated.) Plato says that Agathon had polished manners, wealth, wisdom and dispensed hospitality with ease and refinement.

Herodian wrote a history of Greece entitled *History of the Empire from the Death of Marcus*, in eight books. Thanks to him we learn a great deal about Elagabalus.

Herodotus was contemporary to some of the events that interest us here. Cicero called him the Father of History, while Plutarch wrote that he was the Father of Lies. His masterpiece is *The Histories*, considered a chef-d'oeuvre, a work that the gods have preserved intact right up to our own day, a divine intervention that would not have surprised a believer like Herodotus (it's also a book I reread every year). Part of his work may have been derived from other sources (what historian's work isn't?) and the facts rearranged in an effort to give them dramatic force and please an audience. Much of what he did was based on oral histories, many of which themselves were based on early folk tales, highly suspect, naturally, in all their details. Aristophanes made fun of segments of his work and Thucydides called Herodotus a storyteller. Surprisingly little is known about his own life. For example, he writes lovingly about Samos, leading some to believe that he may have spent his youth there. Born near Ionia, he wrote in that dialect, learning it perhaps on Samos. He was his own best publicist, taking his works to festivals and games, such as the Olympic Games, and reading them to the spectators. As I've said, many people doubt that he actually went where he said he went and saw what he said he saw. But the same was true of Marco Polo who causes disbelief to this day simply because he never mentioned eating noodles in China or seeing the Great Wall or even drinking Chinese tea. No historian, then as now, can write a book on ancient occurrences without referring to Herodotus' observations. An amusing example of recent discoveries that give credence to Herodotus is this: Herodotus wrote about a kind of giant ant, the size of a fox, living in India, in the desert, that dug up gold. This was ridiculed until the French ethnologist Peissel came upon a marmot living in today's Pakistan that burrows in the sand and has for generations brought wealth to the region by bringing up gold from its burrows. Peissel suggests that the original confusion came from the fact that the Persian word for marmot was similar to the word for mountain ant.

Isocrate was a student of Socrates who wrote a speech in the defense of Alcibiades during a trial that took place after his death.

Josephus, 37 A.D. to around 100 A.D., was a historian born in Jerusalem. He fought against the Romans and was captured by Vespasian who kept him as his interpreter and, later, Josephus even assumed the emperor's family name, becoming a citizen (Titus Flavius Josephus). A Jew, he turned against his people and helped Vespasian's son Titus to loot the Second Temple. His works include *The Jewish War* and *Antiquities of the Jews.*

Juvenal was a satirical poet who wrote *Satires.*

Lucan (Marcus Annaeus Lucanus) lived from 39 A.D. to 65 A.D., a short life due to his being ordered by Nero to commit suicide because of his role in the treasonous Piso conspiracy. In hopes of a pardon, he implicated his mother among others, all of whom followed him in death. He was a poet, a close friend of Nero until the emperor grew tired of him and his poetry, after which Lucan's writing became insulting, insults Nero was said to have ignored.

Lysias was extremely wealthy and contemporary with Alcibiades. He founded a new profession, logographer, which consisted of writing speeches delivered in law courts. One of his speeches was *Against Andocides*, another was *Against Alcibiades.*

Memmius was an orator and poet, and friend of Pompey but eventually went over to Caesar.

Mimnermus was born in Ionian Smyrna around 630 B.C. He wrote short love poems suitable for performance at drinking parties.

Myron of Priene is the author of a historical account of the First Messenian War.

Pausanias, a Greek historian and geographer, famous for his *Description of Greece.* He was contemporary with Hadrian and Marcus

Aurelius. He's noted as being someone interested in everything, careful in his writing and scrupulously honest.

Phanocles lived during the time of Alexander the Great. He was the author of a poem on boy-love that described the love of Orpheus for Calais, and his death at the hands of Thracian women.

Philemon lived to be a hundred but alas only fragments of his works remain. He must have been very popular as he won numerous victories as a poet and playwright.

Pindar's great love was Theoxenus of Tenodos about whom he wrote: "Whosoever, once he has seen the rays flashing from the eyes of Theoxenus, and is not shattered by the waves of desire, has a black heart forged of a cold flame. Like wax of the sacred bees, I melt when I look at the young limbs of boys." He lived around 500 B.C. and celebrated the Greek victories against the Persians at Salamis and Plataea. His home in Thebes became a must for his devotees.

Plato was a major source for this book, along with Xenophon, Thucydides and Plutarch. Plato's most famous work is the Allegory of the Cave. Humans in the cave have no other reality than the shadows they see on the walls. If they looked around, they could see what was casting the shadows and by doing so gain additional knowledge. If they left the cave they would discover the sun, analogous to truth. If those who saw the sun reentered the cave and told the others, they would not be believed. There are thusly different levels of reality that only the wisest are able to see; the others remain ignorant. It's basically thanks to Plato and Xenophon that we know what we do about Socrates. Plato's perfect republic is ruled by the best (an aristocracy), headed by a philosopher king who guides his people thanks to his wisdom and reason. An inferior form of government, one that comes after an aristocracy, is a timocracy, ruled by the honorable. A timocracy is in the hands of a warrior class. Plato has Sparta in mind, but it's unclear how he could have found this form of government better than, for example, a democracy. The problem may be that we know, in reality, so little about Sparta. Next comes an oligarchy based on wealth, followed by a democracy, rule by just anyone and everyone. This degenerates into a tyranny, meaning a government of oppression, because of the conflict between the rich and the poor in a democracy.

Pliny the Younger was the Elder's nephew. He witnessed the explosion of Vesuvius. He was a lawyer and a letter writer, many of which remain, vital historical sources of the times. His letters concerning Trajan are of special importance. Under Trajan he worked side by side with Suetonius.

Plutarch was born near Delphi around 46 A.D. to a wealthy family. He was married, and a letter to his wife even exists to this day. He had sons, the exact number unknown. He studied mathematics and philosophy in Athens and was known to have visited most of the major Greek sites mentioned in this book, as well as Rome. He personally knew the Emperors Trajan and Hadrian, and became a Roman citizen. He was a high priest at Delphi and his duty consisted of interpreting the auguries of the Pythoness (no mean task). He wrote the *Lives of the Emperors* but alas only two of the lesser emperors survive. Another verily monumental work was *Parallel Lives of Greeks and Romans* of which twenty-three exist. His interest was the destinies of his subjects, how they made their way through the meanders of life, the Jekyll/Hyde struggle of virtue versus vice. A small jest, he went on, often reveals more than battles during which thousands die. His writings on Sparta, alongside those of Xenophon, are nearly all we possess concerning that extraordinary city-state. His major biographies are the *Life of Alexander* and the *Life of Julius Caesar*. Amusingly, Plutarch wrote a scathing review of Herodotus' work in which he stated that the great historian was fanatically biased in favor of the Greeks who could do, according to Herodotus, no wrong.

No gratitude can ever be enough for what this man has given us, although in the case of the Greeks we must never forget that he was writing *500 years after the events*.

Polybius, around 200 B.C. to 118 B.C., was a Greek historian whose *The Histories* covered the period from 264 to 146 B.C. He was a friend of Scipio Africanus. He details the ascent to empire of Rome, and was present at the destruction of Carthage.

Polyenus was a Macedonian known as a rhetorician and for his books on war strategies.

Sallust was a Roman historian and politician, 86 B.C. to about 35 B.C. One of his works concerned Catiline and he wrote *Histories* of which only fragments remain.

Seneca (Lucius Annaeus Seneca) lived around 4 B.C. to 65 A.D. He was the advisor of Caligula, Claudius and Nero who forced him to commit suicide for supposedly planning his overthrow. He is known for his philosophical essays, letters and tragedies.

Simonides of Ceos was a Greek poet born about 550 B.C. Besides his poems, he added four letters to the Greek alphabet.

Suetonius (Gaius Suetonius Tranquillus) lived around 69 A.D. to 123 A.D. He was a truly great Roman historian known for his *Twelve Caesars*, his only extant work. Pliny the Younger says that he was studious and totally dedicated to writing. He was highly favored by both Trajan, under whom he served as his secretary, and Hadrian who fired him for having an affair with the Empress Vibia Sabina.

Sophocles was the author of 123 plays of which 7 remain, notably *Oedipus* and *Antigone*. An Athenian born to a rich family just before the Battle of Marathon, he was a firm supporter of Pericles. He fought alongside Pericles against Samos when the island attempted to become autonomous from Athens. He was elected as a magistrate during the Sicilian Expedition led by Alcibiades, and given for function the goal of finding out why the expedition had ended disastrously. Sophocles was always ready and willing to succumb to the charms of boys. Plutarch tells us that even at age 65 ''Sophocles led a handsome boy outside the city walls to have his way with him. He spread the boy's poor himation--a rectangular piece of cloth thrown over the left shoulder that drapes the body--upon the ground. To cover them both he spread his rich cloak. After Sophocles took his pleasure the boy took the cloak and left the himation for Sophocles. This misadventure was eventually known to all.'' He died at 90, some say while reciting a very long tirade from *Antigone* because he hadn't paused to take a breath. Another version has him choking on grapes, and a final one has him dying of happiness after winning the equivalent of our Oscar at a festival. The first of his trilogy--called the Theban plays--is *Oedipus the King*. Here the baby Oedipus--in a plot that goes back to Priam and Paris at the founding of Troy--is handed over to a servant to be killed in order to prevent the accomplishment of an oracle, an oracle stating that he will kill his father and marry his mother. He does both after solving the riddle of the sphinx (which creature becomes four-footed, then two-footed and finally three-footed?). His mother, when she finds out she's been bedding her own son, commits suicide and Oedipus blinds himself. In *Oedipus at Colonus* Oedipus dies and we learn more about his children Antigone, Polyneices and Eteocles. In *Antigone* Polyneices is accused of treason and killed. His body is thrown outside the city walls and the king forbids its burial, under pain of death. Antigone does so anyway and, faced with death, she commits suicide, followed by the king's son who was going to wed her, followed by the king's wife who couldn't face losing her precious son. (Whew!)

Tacitus, around 56 A.D. to 117 A.D., was a historian who wrote *Annals* and *Histories*, concerning Tiberius, Claudius, Nero and the Year of the Four Emperors. He is known for his insights into the psychology of his subjects.

Theocritus was a Sicilian and lived around 270 B.C. In his 7th Idyll Aratus is passionately in love with a lad. His 12th Idyll refers to Diocles who died saving the life of Philolaus, the boy he loved, and in whose honor kissing contests were held every spring at his tomb. In his 23rd Idyll a lover commits suicide because of unrequited love, warning his belovèd that one day he too will burn and weep for a cruel boy. Before hanging himself the lover kissed the doorpost from which he would attach the noose. The boy treated the corpse with disdain and went off to the gymnasium for a swim where a statue of Eros fell on him, coloring the water with his blood. In his 29th Idyll a lover warns his belovèd that he too will age and his beauty will lose its freshness. He is therefore advised to show more kindness as ''you will one day be desperate for a beautiful young man's attentions.'' Although lads are often disappointing, it is impossible not to fall madly in love with them. In the 30th Idyll the poet states that when a man grows old he should keep a distance from boys, but in his heart he knows that the only alternative to loving a boy is simply to cease to exist.

Theognis was born around 550 B.C. His poems consist of maxims and advice as to how to live life. Fortunately, a great deal of his work has come down to us, most of which is dedicated to his belovèd, the handsome Cyrnus.

Thucydides was an Athenian general and historian, contemporary with the events he described. What he wrote was based on what actually happened; there was no extrapolating; no divine intervention on the part of the gods as was the case with Plutarch. An example of this was his observation that birds and animals that ate plague victims died as a result, leading him to conclude that the disease had a natural rather than supernatural cause. His description of the plague has never been equaled, the plague that he himself caught while participating in the Peloponnesian War. He is thought to have died in 411 B.C., the date at which his writing suddenly stops. He admired Pericles and democracy but not the radical form found in Athens.

Tyrtaeus, a rare Spartan writer, left us an account of the Second Messenian War. The purpose of his poetry was to inspire Spartan support of the Spartan state. Athenians claimed he was of Athenian birth. Pausanias maintained that the Athenians had sent him to Sparta as an insult, because he was both crazy, lame and had one eye. Herodotus wrote that he was only one of two foreigners to be given Spartan citizenship.

Xenophon, born near Athens in 430 B.C., was a historian and general. His masterpieces are *The Peloponnesian Wars* and *Anabasis.* He loved Sparta and served under Spartan generals during the Persian Wars. Like the Spartans, he believed in oligarchic rule, rule by the few, be they the most intelligent or wealthy or militarily acute. He spent a great deal of time in Persia alongside Cyrus the Younger who raised an army, among whom were Xenophon's 10,000 and other mercenaries (all of which is the subject of *Anabasis*). After Cyrus' death Xenophon and his ten thousand made their way back home, the breathtaking account of which ends his *Anabasis.* The Athenians exiled him when he fought with the Spartans against Athens but the Spartans offered him an estate where he wrote his works. His banishment may have been revoked thanks to his son Gryllus who brilliantly fought and died for Athens.

OTHER SOURCES

(1) See my book *The Origin of Orgies.*
(2) See my book *Roman Homosexuality* for the full history of Carthage.
(3) See my book *SPARTA.*

(4) What followed can be found in my book *Roman Homosexuality*.
(5) See my book *Hadrian and Antinous*.
(6) See my book *The Sacred Band of Thebes*.
(7) See my book *Cesare Borgia*.

Abbott Jacob, *History of Pyrrhus*, 2009
Baker Simon, *Ancient Rome*, 2006
Everitt Anthony, *Cicero*, 2001
Everitt Anthony, *Augustus*, 2006
Everitt Anthony, *Hadrian*, 2009
Galassi, Francis, *Catiline*, 2004
Goldsworthy Adrian, *The Fall of Carthage*, 2000
Goldsworthy Adrian, *In the Name of Rome*, 2003
Goldsworthy Adrian, *Caesar*, 2006
Goodman Rob and Soni Jimmy, *Rome's Last Citizen*, 2012
Grant Michael, *History of Rome*, 1978
Harris Robert, *Imperium*, 2006
Holland Tom, *Rubicon*, 2003
Hughes Robert, *Rome*, 2011
Livy, *Rome and the Mediterranean*
Livy, *The War with Hannibal*
Matyszak Philip, *Mithridates the Great*, 2008
McLynn, *Marcus Aurelius*, 2009
Miles Richard, *Carthage Must be Destroyed*, 2010
Miles Richard, *Ancient Worlds*, 2010
Opper Thorsten, *Hadrian*, 2008
Polybius, *The Histories*
Renucci Pierre, *Caligula*, 2000
Sallust, *The Conspiracy of Catiline*, Penguin Classics, 1963
Schiff, Stacy, *Cleopatra*, 2010
Strauss Barry, *The Spartacus War*, 2009
Suetonius, *The Twelve Caesars*
Tacitus, *The Annals of Imperial Rome*
Tacitus, *The Histories*
Tibullus, The Elegies of Tibullus, translated by Theodore C. Williams
Ward-Perkins Bryan, *The Fall of Rome*, 2005
Wheaton James, *Spartacus*, 2011
Wikipedia: Research today is impossible without the aid of this monument.
Williams Craig A. *Roman Homosexuality*, 2010
Williams John, *Augustus*, 1972

INDEX

Please note that the page numbers are *passim*. An example, Cato 76 –
102 means that Cato is found within these pages, but not necessarily on
every page.

Zoticus 67-89

Printed in Great Britain
by Amazon

49991494R00088